The Recovery of Preaching

HARPER'S MINISTERS PAPERBACK LIBRARY

The Recovery of Preaching

HENRY H. MITCHELL

Published in San Francisco by

HARPER & ROW, PUBLISHERS

New York, Hagerstown, San Francisco, London

To all my spiritual ancestors in Africa and America,

Especially my grandparents:

    Rev. Henry H. Mitchell (1852–1940)
    Laura Parsons Mitchell (18 –1921)
    Rev. Henry Estis   (1862–1948)
    Elizabeth Lewis Estis   (1871–1935)

And my parents:

    Orlando W. Mitchell   (1886–1966)
    Bertha Estis Mitchell   (1892–1973)

THE RECOVERY OF PREACHING

Copyright © 1977 by Henry H. Mitchell

Designed by Jim Mennick

Library of Congress Cataloging in Publication Data

Mitchell, Henry H.
    The recovery of preaching.
    Includes bibliographical references.
    1. Preaching—Addresses, essays, lectures.
I. Title.
BV4222.M5   251   76-62959
ISBN 0-06-065763-4

81 10 9 8 7 6 5 4 3

Contents

Acknowledgements

THIS WORK is the result of creativity, encouragement, and help from several sources. First of all, I am indebted to the Black preaching tradition itself, and to all the fathers and mothers of the faith who together adapted and created and molded a heritage of deep and powerful religious communication. Nor can I forget the contemporary exponents of the tradition, too numerous to mention by name, whom I have observed and studied so carefully in my own pilgrimage of reclaiming and defining it. In that process I have been richly assisted, also, by classes of preachers at Colgate Rochester Divinity School/Bexley Hall/Crozer Theological Seminary, The School of Theology at Claremont [California], Fuller Theological Seminary at Pasadena, and the Ecumenical Center for Black Church Studies, where every semester sees one or two classes launched in preaching.

Portions of this material have also been presented at various times at The Virginia College and Seminary, Lynchburg; The School of Theology at Virginia Union University, Richmond; and the Yale University Divinity School, with the first four chapters being edited from my presentations there for the 1974 Lyman Beecher Lectures on Preaching. I owe a great debt of gratitude to the Yale faculty, students and alumni for constraining me to deal more seriously with what the Black preaching tradition has to say outside its culture. In addition, Richard Lucas of Harper & Row is responsible for suggesting the still more detailed application and extension of my understandings of the tradition, resulting in the last five chapters. His encouragement was crucial.

Technically speaking, much credit goes to Mrs. Jeanne Anderson for struggling through six chapters of cassette dictation, and to Ella, my devoted wife, whose quiet, patient, methodical assistance was monumental. But far beyond her proofing and critiques was the incalculable value of her inexhaustibly supportive spirit.

The result is what I hope may be a widely helpful analysis of the genius of Black preaching, in terms that are understandable alike to White and Black, clergy and laity. As always, I see it as only a beginning of a sharing process that will enrich the pulpit of all cultures.

What I have accomplished, if anything, required the multigenerational contribution and assistance of hosts of hearts and heads and hands. What I have failed to achieve is my own responsibility.

HENRY H. MITCHELL

Claremont, California
September 30, 1976

1. An Introductory Sermon

THE MESSAGE of this book is perhaps best summed up in the sermon which was the fourth of the 1974 Lyman Beecher Lectures at Yale Divinity School. It is here transcribed as preached two years later in the Annual Bible Conference at Massanetta Springs, a conference center of the Presbyterian Church, U.S., Synod of the Virginias.

TO SIT WHERE THEY SIT

Then I came to them of the captivity at Tel-Abib, that dwelt by the river of Chebar, and I sat where they sat, and remained there astonished among them seven days.

EZEKIEL 3:15

If somebody were to ask you what is the hardest job in the Kingdom of God, what would you answer? What *is* the hardest job in the Kingdom of God? I know a lot of people who would say parent to a teenager; there is no harder job in the world. I know some others who would say, teacher in the inner-city schools, for there is no more difficult task anywhere than that of trying to teach children with the difficulties which some of them have had to suffer. I know some people who would say that the hardest job in the world is to be a pastor of a church, any church. And quite a few others would say, the hardest job is not the pastor's, but the pastor's wife, because she has all that responsibility and no authority. And there are some among us who would say the toughest job in the world is to be a teenager in the midst of all of these crazy adults.

Now all of these people are right in a sense, and all of their tasks are hard because of two major problems, one of which is rapid social change. All of us have assigned roles, and our roles are changing so rapidly that most of us haven't the slightest idea of what we are supposed to be doing or what is expected of us. The other thing that comes upon us is the difficulty of communicating. Once these roles get all shuffled together we have an increasing problem of communication. Now, quite frankly, I can't change the rate of change; I can't slow it down. But all of us can improve our abilities to communicate, and to this end it is instructive to watch Ezekiel, whose contribution to us may be summed up in five words of our text from Ezekiel 3:15, "I sat where they sat." "Then I came to them of the captivity that dwelt by the river Chebar, and I sat where they sat and remained there astonished or in a trance among them for seven days." This is the last verse of a lengthy account of his call, and, strangely enough, what he says occurred to him in this vision actually took many, many years for him to accomplish in fact.

His pilgrimage is typical of many of our pilgrimages. He was a young priest, he had very high ideals, he was committed to some great abstractions, some great principles, if you please, and reality was unusually traumatic for him. From a youthful, all-out admiration for Josiah and his great religious reforms, he went to bitter disillusionment when he was exiled along with the cream of the Jews of his time. From membership in a respected family of ruling priests, he went to an exile in which his people had very fluctuating rights. There was no right which was guaranteed to them, for they were expatriates. They were not slaves, but they surely were not free. They were not really able to speak of themselves as their own, and this was a far cry from being a member of a powerful family of priests.

He went from a youthful and probably full-time ministry in

the air-conditioned hills of Zion, to what was at best a bivocational ministry among the tillers of a sweltering, watery wasteland along a manmade navigable channel of the river Euphrates. He went from presiding in a beautiful temple atmosphere at Jerusalem to the very difficult task of organizing impromptu gatherings down by a river, where dispirited exiles found it hard to sing the songs of Zion in a strange land and without a building. Perhaps worst of all, from a secure base in the center of orthodoxy—from easy certainty inside the very normative school of thought of his time—he went to trying to speak to an audience who considered themselves transients. They were apartment dwellers; they were housing-project types; they were hoping soon to go home; and they were divided between the numbing grief of forced expatriation and the temptation to seek the strength of the Gods of their conquerors.

Anyone who has ever preached to transient people knows that you are preaching to a parade, and it is a difficult thing at best. Few young priests have had it so hard as Ezekiel had it. Ezekiel said he sat astonished seven days, and I used to mistake his vision for the first week in the new parish. I had the bright idea that what he was giving as a vision was what actually happened. Scholars say that this is not so, that when he went in his earlier years to Babylonia, he never went back to Jerusalem. He was in a *trance* seven days while God dealt with him, several years after he had moved to Babylonia. Here was a young man who saw himself in inflated, idealistic terms, a young man who was full of the cult of Josiah, whether they had followed it or not, who had it all nailed down. It was right, it was orthodox, it was the "in" thing, and in this vision he tried to resist the realities of the nitty-gritty situation by the river Chebar. In the vision and in actual life he was a judgmental prophet of scathing pronouncement, as most young preachers fancy themselves to be. And his chief concerns, as you read the book, are for Jerusalem and the temple and for all of those very well-established traditions in which he fancied lay all salvation.

As he says in the vision just before our text, he was resisting in the heat of his spirit, and he was compelled of God to become a priest-prophet. He was *made* by God to identify with the needy, hurting people of whom he himself, had he only stopped to think, must have been numbered as one. He did then, not in the vision but in the history which unfolded thereafter, what he was supposed to do. He did in fact begin to sit where they sat, and strangely enough he did so only after the destruction of Jerusalem.

The pilgrimage of his preaching and the softening of his spirit are really fascinating to watch. Under the guidance of the spirit of God he broke tradition and waxed creative and sent forth some brilliant new understandings of what God is about and what God would have us do. He heard them saying, for instance, that the sins of their fathers were what caused them to be where they were. He was quite forthright about it all when he said, "You've heard it said that your fathers have eaten sour grapes and the children's teeth are on edge." He said, "I want you to do away with this foolishness; no more let this be said in Israel. 'As the soul of the father is Mine, so also is the soul of the son, and the soul that sins, *that's* the one that's going to die.' Not somebody else, the soul that *commits* the sin, that's the one that is going to die." In so proclaiming he began the roots of individual responsibility which are so strong, perhaps even too strong, for we think not enough of corporate responsibility in our times. In this creative pilgrimage, Ezekiel proclaimed a kind of liturgical liberty which had never been known before. He made it plain that you don't absolutely have to be where the Ark of the Covenant is; you don't have to be at the temple itself. And he declared, at the end of his ministry, God's willingness, God's promise to put his spirit *within* you. The clarification is, "I'll put my spirit in you *wherever* you are; you don't have to be on the top of Mount Zion."

In the process of this declaration, Ezekiel comes forth with the magnificent doctrine or the beginnings of the doctrine of what we now call Grace—the willingness of God to deal with us and to bless us and make us acceptable regardless of how far we have strayed away. In keeping with this, of course, he declared that vision so precious to my people—that of the dry bones. Ever since I was a little fellow I have sung that song, "The kneebone connected to the thighbone." But behind this vivid picture was his tremendous hope, hope that people as dead as dry bones, as bleached dry bones in the desert, can actually be brought to spiritual life again. On the whole, Ezekiel's makeshift ministry to a scattered and dispirited people evolved into what we now know as synagogues, an extremely important preparation for the diaspora. For without this understanding that God can be worshiped and studied in any place, our whole faith might have long since been dead.

During the vision early in his ministry, one gets the feeling that people were busy tuning Ezekiel out—that nobody was listening. But then there is in the thirty-third chapter, after Ezekiel began to really sit where they sat, the report that people said come and listen. "Come and hear; this man has something to say that matches our needs. Come and hear this man; he has something to say that relates to us, that we can understand, something that will help us." Ezekiel is careful to suggest in his record that they didn't do what he said to do, but he is aware in spite of his own slight resistance that people are at last listening to him. I submit that this change came about because he finally sat where they sat, and I submit that the gaps in the understandings on this polarized planet can be closed in very much the same way.

What is that way? Well, it may be summed up with five little ideas. One is to identify with persons, those that you are out to conquer. I get a little tired of people talking about conquering for Christ. I dislike a lot of the implications there. We need to be more like Ezekiel who finally *joined* them. He wasn't ever sent to beat them, he wasn't sent to conquer them, he was sent to be one of them. In so doing he had to avoid contrast, and we must avoid contrast. The signals of difference between ourselves and those whom we serve are many of them unessential, and all of them are signals of distance between us and those to whom we go. We must be constantly sensitive and aware that wherever no great principle is involved, we must identify with the people we serve.

When I say we must identify with them, it may better be summed up, we must stand *with* them and not against them. Prophets though we be, we must be prophets within and not outside of the communities in which we serve.

I taught this last quarter at Fuller Theological Seminary in Pasadena a course on "Black Culture and World View." I had, as perhaps many of you might predict, my greatest resistance to the understanding of our culture from people *within* the culture presumably. One class member in his early fifties or late forties was always kind, but he resisted terribly the idea that there was in fact this tremendous Black difference at points. Then suddenly he changed. I discovered that it had come about because he had had a tremendous, warming, wonderful encounter with his own teenagers. As he struggled with these new ideas they said to him, "That's right on Dad, that's exactly where we are, let's face it." When Daddy faced it, and Daddy stood with them in a situation to which they were far more sensitive than he was—when he stood *with* them—he suddenly discovered that he had great rapport with teenagers. Up to that time they had said of him, "He wears a necktie all day, every day, and he identifies with the very people who crush us most often."

All of us must learn the same lesson that this minister learned, that you must stand with the people whom you serve. Of course Ezekiel had been to school. He was from the ultimate source of wisdom and tradition, and one must use the school's insight. But even as one uses those insights one must forsake identification with those institutions, as opposed to the institutions of which the people themselves are a part.

I'm the director of a center out in Los Angeles, called the Ecumenical Center for Black Church Studies. Perhaps the most important difference between us and any other institution for theological training is not so much what we study in terms of a particular group of people, but the fact that we want at every point to have professors who are also pastors. We do not want to train people who all the rest of their lives are identified with professors and aspire to professorship, rather than identifying with pastors, aspiring to be shepherds of the flock—aspiring above all to serve laity. You can't sit where they sit if you've always got your eye off somewhere on a professorship. All too many people have been misfitted because that's really what they've been programmed for.

We have to sit where they sit, and therefore to see from their perspective. We may have to correct that perspective considerably, but we have to start dealing with *their* issues inside *their* skin and not from some alien identity. The people who go forth must remember what Ezekiel eventually had to remember, that these people are struggling, that they are like the children of Israel who said, "How can we sing the songs of Zion in a strange land?" They said, "We love Israel, we love Judah, we love the temples, we wish we could be there. If we ever forget, let our right hand be cut off. But let it be understood that it's tough trying to serve God under the circumstances where we now operate." And everybody who would reach people who in their feeble and stumbling ways are trying to sing the songs of Zion in the strange and changing ways of our time must know that at least they are trying. We must sit where they sit and help them.

No person of any group, whether of age, race, social or economic status, or nationality, is exempt from the obligation to sit where those "other" people sit. Whoever you are, however alienated you may be, your only hope is to take upon yourself that same obligation that was upon Ezekiel. I preached a sermon many years ago under the title "Hypocrites Anonymous." I indicated that in Alcoholics Anonymous people have to admit, all of them, that they are alcoholic, or they can't really be helped. And I suggested that all of us are hypocrites, and we might as well admit it. If we had a church called Hypocrites Anonymous, we'd have a pretty sound starting place because we are all hypocrites. If we once admit that none of us live up to the obligations of the ideals that we say we believe in, then we could at least be honest, and that's mighty healthy. Well, I was socking it to the old folks, and there were about thirty-five youngsters in the choir behind me. They were rooting for me, because I was saying how old folks claimed to believe many principles they didn't actually practice. All those kids were having a great time, until I turned around and said, "Well they aren't the only hypocrites. I have a suspicion that if I asked most of you where you were last night, Saturday night at twelve o'clock, I might get a 20 percent accurate response. The rest of you would lie just as fast as you could put it together."

I suspect it was one of the most growing experiences most of those young people had ever had. It suddenly dawned on them that they were busy saying that everybody over thirty was a hypocrite, and yet they themselves would never try to defend their own behavior. It wasn't that they were doing things that were unconventional, but they believed in them. They were doing things that were both unconventional *and* wrong, and they *knew* it. Seventeen years old or no seventeen years old, they too were hypocrites. If all of us could sit where "those other people" sit, if those teenagers could see how ridiculous their behavior is from the perspective of adults, and if the adults could see how difficult it is to be a teenager in these times, a great deal could be accomplished.

No group is exempt from the obligation to "sit where they sit," and all groups react positively in the main to people who identify with them. A friend of mine preached a funeral recently for a very prominent, activist Civil Rights person. He was not a member of the church; he was an outspoken nonmember and a critic of the church—a scathing critic of the institution. His mourners, some thousand or twelve hundred of them, were militant and agnostic and even addicts. And the preacher, who was sensitive about what this man's very important life was all about, tried to sit where the deceased sat. He tried to proclaim that part of the gospel which the deceased had unreservedly committed his life to, for his life was dedicated to those things that are pleasing to God in many respects. He said after the funeral that he never wished so much in his life that he were back in the pastorate of a church. Out of that host of people, at least fifty folk had sought him out and said to him, despite all their rhetoric against the church, "Where's your church, where's your church, I want to come and hear you preach." And all they were saying was that for once the preacher who did the eulogy had not stuck his finger in their face and proclaimed a lot of platitudes. Instead he had grappled with the selfsame issues with which they were struggling. He had done so as one of them, not as an enemy.

Many of you will say of course that's too much to ask. "You tell me to sit where they sit, join those guys. Man, that's risky!" And it is risky. But he who calls us never preached from the privacy and protection of a high picket fence. In my world there is a paraphrase of a portion of the Parable of the Vineyard and the Wicked Tenant, and it goes something like this:

In the halls of heaven God the Father called a conference one day to review the progress of communication with the beings on the planet earth; reports were given. There was a report given on the patriarchs, but the report was not good. There was another report given on the judges, but it was not significantly better. There was another report on the kings, and it really was poor. There was a report on the priests and a final report on the prophets, and all of them somehow had failed to communicate. At the close of the report—the evidence that all had failed—God looked to his right. And before he could ask, his son said, "I'll close the gap; I'll try to reconcile them. I'm going to use a different method. I'm going to go and sit where they sit. And if they sit in temptation, I'll sit in temptation." Somebody said he was tempted in all things like as we. "If they sit in hunger, I'll sit in hunger." And they all record that afterwards he was in hunger from forty days of fasting. "If they sit in thirst, I'll sit in thirst." And on the cross it was that he said, "I thirst." "If they sit under a cloud of misunderstanding, I'll sit under a cloud of misunderstanding." And somebody reported that he looked up wistfully one day and said, "Will ye also go away?" "If they sit in sorrow and tears, I'll sit in sorrow and tears." And the shortest verse says that "Jesus wept." "If they sit in deep depression, and if they feel abandoned by God himself, I will sit where they sit." And from the cross he cried, "My God, My God, why hast thou forsaken me?"

Jesus sat where we sit, and we who would serve him in any capacity, we who would reach anybody, must learn also to join them. Wherever they are, we must be one of them, to see, to be astonished if you please, and then to declare what it is God would have us each do.

Let us pray:

Father, we who have divided the world up into the goodies and the baddies—we who have decided all too soon who is with you and who is against you—we who have cut ourselves off from those among whom we need most to minister, beg thy forgiveness. Give us with deep sensitivity and wisdom and understanding and love to join our alienated children and parents, parishioners and people everywhere. Give us the grace to be *with* them and to accept them, and so to relate to them, that they may see thee, and give thee the glory. Amen.

2. Preaching as Folk Culture

THE RECOVERY of preaching in America is heavily dependent on the willingness and ability of preachers to sit where their people sit, existentially and culturally. A working model of the effective communication of the gospel inside the life situation and common culture of the hearing folk is to be found in the preaching tradition of Blackamerican religion. That tradition is examined here for what it may have to contribute to the American pulpit at large.

Black preaching style is a product in large part of a confluence of cultures beginning with African roots, because the everyday culture of the masses of Blackamericans is intimately involved and extremely important in their preaching tradition. Their sermons have been in the folk-cultural mode, and they have had great impact and given great support and guidance in both communal and individual life. By way of contrast it may at least be argued that this has not been true of White middle-class Protestant preaching, which has been carried on in an academically oriented counterculture to the folk idiom of America's majority. Whatever peculiar genius Black preaching may have is in cultural terms largely attributable to its fidelity to its non-European and nonacademic folk roots. These were maintained by the peculiar experience of oppression and separateness forced on Blacks. However, the insights which can be extracted from the study of this cultural process and product have much wider significance.

To approach Black cultural rootedness in any depth requires some agreement about what goals or targets are addressed and about some appropriate terms from the alien Euro-American vocabulary with which to carry on a meaningful conversation. The culture and its preaching tradition may then be historically traced, before final attention is addressed in this chapter to the implications of this history for preaching generally.

THE TARGET OF BLACK PREACHING

In dealing with preaching as rooted in folk culture, the first and perhaps most basic question is that of what part of humankind we seek to address. The obvious answers would seem to be in categories such as race, culture, class, caste, education, and income. But the prior question which applies to all of these categories is, "To what *aspect* of all these persons do we preach? To what process(es) of personality is the gospel directed?" All hope of redemptive communication hangs on whether or not we can reach and touch the decisive processes.

Black preaching assumes a target of whole persons. The largely cerebral appeal of most White preaching would seem to imply a primarily intellectual target, with the homiletic skills sought and taught focusing on the production of a stimulating idea. In contrast to this I see in the African-American continuum of religious experience and practice an answer that lies in the *combination* of the intellectual with the less rational but equally valid processes. We sometimes refer to them as feelings, and we sometimes think that they are void of solid content. But we must preach to the combination in varying emphasis or balance. While *all* human communication partakes of the emotional or the appeal to the less rationally conscious, the best of the Black preaching tradition has synthesized the appeal to the conscious and the so-called unconscious with a unique clarity and intensity.

The presupposition that persons are controlled by their reason has long been held suspect. The existentialists have delivered the philosophical coup de grace, but the practices of many preachers do not reflect this awareness. The advertiser, for instance, uses this insight to much greater advantage. One great reason for the failure to develop a definitive response to emotion has been that feelings in Western culture have somehow been declared unworthy, and those who deal with them are charged with being manipulators. It is conceded that the feelings cast the decisive vote in the unfortunately framed contest between a feelingless brain and a brainless set of feelings. But the person who successfully addresses the feeling-majority in the human centers of decision is often considered unprincipled.

Black culture of the masses has not progressed to the level of this lofty and ancient mistake. The earlier Greek dichotomy of flesh and spirit was perhaps only made worse by the Enlightenment, which added reason-vs.-feeling to the division of the human psyche. But the religious tradition of the Blackamerican does not trace back through this traumatic schism of personality, and so Blacks have emerged into this modern era with a kind of wholeness which is typical of so-called primitive cultures. Thus the best of Black preaching is able to integrate the best of modern insights into this happy Afro-American throwback to wholeness. The prehistoric oneness of conscious and so-called unconscious survives sufficiently well in Black culture, therefore, to give religious, healing access to both "levels" at one and the same time, in a rich tradition of *experience* fused with *content.*

This immediately suggests that Black Religion is far more involved with the nonrational than most Westerners have thought true religion to be. But rather than having a mindless emotional rite, Black religion integrates the content in all sectors of consciousness. In modern America, the content of the Black person's *"un*conscious" may very well be considered as theologically higher than the more manipulable and vulnerable beliefs one has reasoned out. Deep feelings towards God persist among many formally trained Blacks long after the hypocrisy of White Christian Americans and the pseudorationality of their schools have rendered them cynical and nontheistic in the rational sector. The process at work here bears more detailed consideration.

People keep vast collections of responses and values in the less-charted sectors of consciousness, invisibly and largely inaccessibly stored. This storehouse has been developed over a period of years, and, in fact, *as culture* has been developed over long centuries. To the extent that traditional responses clearly imply a view of the world, this culture is de facto theological to use a Western term. Beliefs and practices long disallowed in the rational conscious remain dormant but rise to the surface in a crisis. John S. Mbiti has illustrated the process especially well. In Africa converts to Christianity and their children as well are still in the *cultural* stream of traditional Africa. This sets their rational-conscious religion at variance with their African Traditional Religion. Most solve the conflict by staying on good terms with both. They will get the best Western-trained doctor they can, but will have deep misgivings about betting it all on Western medicine. So they will also employ traditional medicine, a mix of centuries-old herbal cures and psychosomatic medicine oft mislabeled witchcraft. Mbiti refers to the Christian or Muslim faith as the "contact" religion, and the one which comes to the surface in a crisis as the "instant" religion. Of the converts, no matter how educated, he reports that their "unconscious life is deeply traditional," clearly indicating that the "unconscious" can and does store religion.[1]

The traditional African religion and culture of captured slaves was not suddenly squelched, and this partly "unconscious" attitude and value bank has maintained a significant continuum. In three hundred years this *cultural* faith has acculturated (as opposed to conscious conversion) to a point which is profoundly Christian. But this is possible only because *it was very largely Christian to start with.* And perhaps the most important single fact in this whole consideration is that Black-americans were thus able to *keep their traditional faith* in adapted form, avoiding a conflict between the new, consciously chosen faith of their slave environment and the old and often unreasoned culture and- world view of their African past. Free of general conflict between sectors of consciousness in Black culture, the basic human quests and hungers which generate religion and respond to revelation are still "primitively" unhidden, not subjected to "civilized" Christian reasons for repression. What is, at least at times, assumed to be mere emotion may very well be an unashamed expression of the soul heritage of a people still wed to aspects of the profound wisdom and faith of their Black ancestors—still healed and helped by the timeless and time-tested interpretations from their peculiar existential stream.

Before tracing the development of this stream I ought to attempt something of a technical translation of this process, starting from the scientific Western terms most nearly approximate. Translation into alien terms is a risk which must be taken if there is to be any fruitful exchange between cultures.

I think first of all of the controversial "collective unconscious" of C. G. Jung.[2] Despite the fact that I disagree with his concept of inherited archetypes, there is something about the subtle values and responses communicated to the young of every culture which amounts to a kind of inevitable social a priori and value inheritance. It becomes the world view with which all of life is interpreted and in which one feels most comfortable long before one knows its rational significance. It is most certainly collective or communal and undeniably innocent of rational consciousness. In this sense the term *collective unconscious* has real meaning and relevance in the interpretation of Black culture and its communication, with Black religious symbols being much alive. However *un*, the negative prefix, is grossly inaccurate and requires replacement, as we shall see.

The historian of religions, Mircea Eliade, dissociates his use of the term *archetype* from that of Jung. What he does mean is suggested in this quotation from his *Patterns in Comparative Religion:*

> And primitive spirituality lives on in its own way not in action, not as a thing man can effectively accomplish, but as a *nostalgia* which creates things that become values in themselves: art, the sciences, social theory, and all the other things to which men will give the whole of themselves.[3]

My own conviction about a serious religious content in the less rational sectors of Black consciousness is thus supported by Eliade. But he uses a term which is even more helpful as a way of abolishing the need for this dichotomy between the conscious and the supposedly unconscious, even though he does not use the term collective *un*conscious.[4] Eliade suggests that world views are generated as the "result of immemorial existential situations,"[5] an idea parallel to my own finding that this culture-borne religious life is in fact a kind of stored *insight.* And he follows up the implications of rationally conscious original input in the historically early stages of world view by coining and using the term *transconscious.*[6] Thus is he careful to avoid a completely secular reading of religious insight as born in an arational unconscious, and to project a model of religious experience/insight which integrates the religious reading of historical experience on the conscious *and* "unconscious" levels. This gives continuity between the sectors and lifts up the highest in religion as being involved in all. Whatever the differences in detail, transconsciousness surely suggests the kind of multichannel awareness and integration of which I speak in the Black religious tradition, and the basis of the highest mystical unity experienced among Black worshipers.

Another type of descriptive tool may be drawn from Transactional Analysis. It proposes that "our earliest experiences, though ineffable, are recorded and do replay in the present."[7] These experiences are said to form a "script," which is explained thus:

We have evidence that, between the ages of three and seven, a child develops a "script" for his future—i.e. a story-line blueprint that determines how he will live the rest of his life—particularly his important relationships, his feelings about himself and his achievements, and the outcome that he will experience as "success," "failure," "I almost made it," "or at least I tried."[8]

Transactional Analysis suggests how one adopts a central emotional position with respect to oneself and others, starting with position 1 below, working through 2, and 3, hopefully, to position 4. Harris lists them thus:

1. I'M NOT OK—YOU'RE OK
2. I'M NOT OK—YOU'RE NOT OK
3. I'M OK—YOU'RE NOT OK
4. I'M OK— YOU'RE OK[9]

Each person under stress reverts automatically to his characteristic position—changeless except by conscious effort.

It occurs to me that this individual view of the unconscious might be applied to the collective world view of Blackamericans, giving them the faith-genius, right through slavery, to believe in the justice and providence of God. In the developmental years of West African culture/religion, it was intuited that "God is OK," and "Life is OK." No amount of absurdity and injustice seemed capable thereafter of discouraging this profound affirmation of the goodness of life. In a crisis, Blackamericans fell back onto or up into this position. There is a sense in which this script is still replayed even though Blacks are still defrauded and exploited and killed. It constitutes a kind of special gift for belief in God and the goodness of human existence. While the question of how it ever got such a solid start in so difficult a continent for survival as Africa may never be answered, the most important question is how such a successful script for survival and liberation was communicated to succeeding generations and lodged just as effectively in their transconscious.

TRADITION: TRANSMITTAL AND TRANSITION

Black preaching was one of the major contributors to the transmittal or communication of the deep-seated affirmation of the goodness of God and life in America. The tradition was and is uniquely equipped to communicate transconsciously and to nourish faith where it persists the longest and often influences life the most. To suggest how this came to be we must first look at how Black Christianity itself came to be, advancing then to the place of preaching in the pilgrimage of the collective transconscious, as it were. Stated another way, let us look at the process of Black religious acculturation and adaptation whereby the masses of Blacks have evolved a profoundly Christian faith and avoided the stereotypical conflicts between an intellectual Euro-Christianity and a "gut level" African tradition, vastly exceeding in wholeness and staying power the so-called White Christians who for so many years have mistakenly thought of themselves as the Black man's main religious tutors.

To begin with, African captives arrived in America bearing a West African religious tradition which was so similar to the Old Testament that the missionaries who went to Africa after the close of the slave trade centered almost exclusively on the New Testament. For all their mistaken tears about the "heathen bowing before wood and stone," they were perceptive enough to know that Christian imperialism could gain very little mileage against the established religions if all they had to offer was a new set of fathers of the faith—such as Abraham, Isaac, and Jacob. They already had five and seven-day creation stories, a female source of evil in the earth paralleling Eve, a flood story, a tower-of-Babel-type myth, and, above all, a High God who was omnipotent, omniscient, and just. The affirmation of the goodness of life and of its Creator was so deep that one of the most popular doctrines in Africa, even now, is that of the providence of God, expressed magnificently in folk culture by proverbs and tales and praise-names for God.

Blacks here in America soon found a level of evil they had

never dreamed of, and they saw so little visible justice in this life that they quite functionally appropriated the local ideas of hell as a place to put "ol' Marse," preserving justice. And they *celebrated* their new idea by singing that everybody talking about heaven wasn't going there. The slaves had no notion that they themselves would miss, however, and they planned to shout all over God's heaven, all in the same Spiritual. With the peril of hell they embraced also a new idea called grace, soon making the hymn "Amazing Grace" their favorite new musical acquisition, after proper Blackenization. Through it all they missed the supportive presence of the extended family so much that they also embraced a newly discovered Jesus, Son of God and intermediary, who had suffered like they suffered, being born in a manger and being denied a fair trial before giving up this life in cruel execution. No longer was God ineffable and distant, with profound transcendence only; he even made himself known and very near in the possession of the Holy Ghost, an experience no longer attributed to a multiplicity of sub-divinities. In short, their African Traditional Religions were a solid base or first old testament on which they built their own authentic folk Christianity in the nearly two hundred years (1619 to 1800s) before it was decided that it was safe and even profitable to assume they had souls and should be evangelized. Whatever the early nineteenth-century missionary efforts accomplished, they certainly did not provide the definitive shape of Black religion. The reporters of the time, especially of the first years of "emancipation," spared no pains in saying how obstinately Blacks clung to what was thought then to be heathenish *African* emotional excess.

How did they go about keeping and communicating their own special brand of culture/religion? Obviously a great deal of this God-trusting world view was communicated in the earliest years, in the limited contact of parents with their children. And obviously those parents had worship customs which nourished both the parents' faith and that of the child. But the pattern of communication suggested here needs spelling out. To offset formal didactic implications one needs to see how faith/culture was communicated in the Motherland. This will also suggest a great deal which is relevant to the Black preaching tradition.

Religion in West Africa is interwoven into all of life, somewhat as it was in pre-Enlightenment Europe, but with a happier and more celebrative style. Contrary to stereotypes of "natives" haunted by fears and superstitions, Africans before slavery *and* today lived and live in a highly supportive extended family community. The stages of life and the agricultural seasons were and are cause for what we would call celebration. At a harvest or a marriage festival, history and wisdom are the order of the day, not in cold speeches but as the subjects of dancing, drumming, singing, and tale-telling. Because the languages are tonal, even the tales might sound to us a bit like a chant. Whatever the presentation, the total community knows it so well that one dare not make a mistake of memory. All have learned the materials well just because they are beamed at them from early childhood on so many "wave lengths" or through so many media. They don't know *when* they learned a given saying, but they know the passage. They listen attentively partly because of the *improvisation* or *style factor*, which lends fresh interest to the recital and fulfills the performer in the artistic satisfaction of having led the family in what is always a group performance/experience. I have seen a festival for the living dead in which very small children were, at points, the stars, turning no-hand flips and acting out a tradition which could only be for them a happy and unforgettable legacy.

. When the nonliteracy of these earlier cultures is viewed askance, one has only to remember that with such accurate mental data banks, there was no real or felt need for print. It is, after all, only a substitute for the human memory and speech. Further, the festive air and total involvement of the community gave this learning process a much greater penetration and retention, backing it all up with what might be called ecstatic reinforcement. The oral tradition of Africa was and is very lively, and yet stable and capable of great retention.

It was with this type of both religious content and communication style that African captives arrived on these shores. As early Black preachers took their texts from their bare hands, open to resemble a Bible held, what seemed prodigious biblical memory was only a quick exchange of similar African and Biblical oral traditions. And what seemed like a chanted sermonic caricature with excessive interruption was in fact a replay of a feast at home, with English oral subtitles. The new language was that of a "Christian" nation, and that made the service "Christian" also. A Black professor at a midwestern college once confessed to me that although he would like to put the Black church out of business, he had also to admit that the sermons he heard in Virginia as a boy were startlingly similar to a fetish sermon he had heard in West Africa the previous summer. While the content of this celebrative style of worship was slowly adapted to a profoundly Christian position, the *style* has persisted with even less acculturative change.

For a few moments let us hazard an hypothesis as to how this transition from folk festival to contemporary Black pulpit took place. The first stage is interestingly recorded by Miles Mark Fisher, gleaned from an earlier primary source, Francis Trollope, who wrote of an incident in Indiana, 1829:

> One of these. . . . was preaching with the most violent gesticulations, frequently springing high from the ground, and clapping his hands over his head. Could our missionary societies have heard the trash he uttered, by way of an address to the Diety, they might perhaps have doubted whether his conversion had much enlightened his mind.[10]

This is typical of White response to the African influence, and, although late in the slave period, an accurate idea of what was taking place in the adaptation of their tradition to the new environment.

There is a sense in which this first stage of the African oral tradition is still alive and well in America. Bruce A. Rosenberg has written a whole book on the contemporary folk preacher, mostly about Blacks, whose repertoire differs from the above only in that the biblical elements have had more years to be acculturated into the style.[11] His study had to do with folk *literature*, Black preaching being a contemporary model of the way *Beowulf* was probably rendered and preserved. As a study of preaching it lacks much, but it does not pretend to be such, accurately diagnosing the folk processes which are still at work in parts of the Black pulpit.

A second stage more directly related to the pulpit practices of White America began early to emerge. The Great Awakening produced White worship which, being "closest to what he had known in Africa,"[12] easily bridged the cultural gap to form the African-American. Thus it provided readily adaptable inputs for the earliest Black preachers. Exslave Gustavus Vassa reported being "very much struck and impressed" with the fervor and earnestness of George Whitefield's preaching in Philadelphia in 1766. Vernon Loggins[13] and William H. Pipes tended to interpret this too literally, and to attribute the Great Awakening's impact on Blacks entirely in terms of emotional intensity. Many other scholars have done the same. Emotional expressiveness was no doubt one of the appealing factors, but Pipes's own commentary[14] provides evidence of two other factors which I think are far more important. The first is a restatement of the "emotional" explanation in terms of the kinship between revivalist or camp meeting *shouting*, and the powerful tradition of possession by the gods or spirits of Africa. The other factor is musicality of delivery, or the English counterpart to the tonality of West African language.

Pipes quotes Benjamin Franklin's report that there were as many as thirty thousand people "at one time swayed by his [Whitefield's] eloquence in an out-of-doors crowd in Philadelphia."[15] This would make me wonder immediately how Whitefield could be heard by so large a crowd without a public address system, except that I know for myself how to use the speaking voice musically, to increase volume without damage to the vocal chords. Franklin confirms this as his account continues, as quoted in Pipes:

> His delivery . . . was so improved by frequent repetition that every accent, every emphasis, every modulation of the voice, was so perfectly well-turned that without being interested in the subject,

one could not help being pleased with the discourse; a pleasure of much the same kind with that received from an excellent piece of music.

Pipes follows Franklin with his own analysis, which includes:

His voice was rich and clear and had a wonderful range [a *musical* term]. Whitefield had perfect voice modulation.

All African speech was characterized by tonality, and to follow Whitefield's preaching example was literally to "go home to African facsimiles," in contrast to the cold and unmodulated utterances of the Anglicans, whose churches had dominated slave territory prior to the harvest of the Great Awakening. The nourishment of identity and the nostalgic appeal of Whitefield-ian preaching was like a drink of water from home.

It is not likely to be mere happenstance then, that the greatest Black preacher, serving the largest Black church in the early history of the Black Church in America, was Andrew Marshall of Savannah, Georgia, Whitefield's headquarters city. Marshall illustrates well this second stage in the adaptation of Black preaching to the American scene. He and others did it so well that one may well wonder if there has ever evolved or been a need for a third stage. He kept the strengths of African tradition and adapted them in the direction of the Whitefield model. Again we can refer to the written report of a British writer, Charles Lyell, who paid a visit to Savannah's First African Baptist Church:

The singing was followed by prayers, not read, but delivered without notes by a Negro of pure African blood, a gray-headed venerable-looking man, with a fine sonorous voice [shades of African tonality], named Marshall.[16]

Lyell was informed that Marshall was one of "their best preachers," and he was greatly impressed by the content of the message. But the point here is that Marshall, like all the emerging breed of bicultural or adaptive preachers, was gifted in the use of a musicality of delivery legitimated by Whitefield, but stemming from the same African source as some of Marshall's best illustration style. (His story of the stirring of the eagle's nest was in the very best African animal-story tradition.)

It is not irrelevant to note here that this appealing style of oral communication, rooted in folk culture, was no doubt a factor in the accurate transgenerational transmittal of the originally oral traditions which we now know as the Old and the New Testaments. And it is equally significant to note that today's technical developments in mass media have helped us to go back to the oral in even such print-oriented fields as public education. The process has come full circle, and the style of Black oral communication is the wave not only of the past but of the future. At the same time, this style is to the Black community not only preachment and worship, but art and (for want of a better word) recreation and celebration. It is the result of African tradition influenced by the Euro-American Christian tradition, not "Christian" influenced by African culture.

RELEVANCE FOR TODAY'S PULPIT

Now what has all this to say about the preaching of men of *all* cultures in today's churches? I have seven suggestions to make. The first stems from a lesson in Black "motherwit" which should be equally obvious to any modern missionary: never fight a war with or engage in frontal attack against the prevalent culture. It is not only unwise to tackle that which is so well entrenched; it is foolish and damaging to the psyche to try to destroy the world view buried so deeply in people that their identity and living wisdom are tied up in it. If and when persons are stripped or bereft of their culture, they become pathologically disoriented, in need of institutional care. Fortunately, very few people are ever successfully stripped of culture and world view.

Black preaching is as effective as it is in the Black community because it has never tried to wage a major war against the culture of the masses of folk. To be sure, the learned Bishop Daniel A. Payne and others tried to wipe out such folk survivals as the ring shout, but they were never in the majority, and they were never successful among the masses. To be sure, also, a great deal of modern and sophisticated wisdom from outside the culture is expressed in Black sermons, but it is always most effectively communicated by translation into the "mother tongue"—the imagery and idiom of the Black masses. Culture, like language, must be taken for granted, as medium rather than content, and no amount of concern for education or for orthodoxy must be allowed to lure one into confrontation with the funded wisdom and style of hundreds of years of a group or race's communal life.

This is not to suggest, however, that culture is automatically sacred and untouchable, or that it is buried too deeply to be changed. Quite to the contrary, there are times when it must be dealt with and altered. But that which is not originally formed in the contemporary rational conscious cannot be changed so easily by those processes. Black preaching has been known to change the stances of whole thousands of people, but it was from *within* the traditional style, and by its genius for dealing transconsciously with the conscious *and* the "unconscious." The better or higher content of the transconscious is thus maintained and enhanced, while the lesser is acculturated slowly away from the less accessible reaches of the unconscious. Or, to return to the terms of Transactional Analysis, there is supplied or strengthened a more Christian script, tape, or reading of the realities of life. Throughout the process of acculturation, the person growing transconsciously does not have to feel that the ancestors' wisdom and one's own identity are under attack. *Acculturation and not intellectual imperialism is the process of preference,* since it operates best on the levels least accessible to rational change.

This insight applies to all peoples everywhere. The White middle-class church suffers today from the fact that its leadership has been taught to scoff at and war against the "less intellectual" world view of the average member. It is this lack of indigenous communication and insight for coping, more than the cost of supposedly heroic prophetic stands on social issues, which has driven so many gifted persons from the ministry. Too many have sacrificed too much trying to deal consciously and intellectually with that which was not naturally amenable to such processes. Thus the editors of most major brand Protestant hymnbooks sought to exterminate old hymns like "Amazing Grace" and "O Happy Day," only to see them burst from the White supposedly unconscious as hit tunes in the pop world, regardless of how poorly performed. The more realistic approach would have been to try a few amendments which would keep the cultural entity intact and alter the content of some of the theologically more obnoxious lyrics. What is true of improving White hymnology is equally true of improving the White pulpit, both as to content and style.

Contemporary fundamentalism leaves much to be desired intellectually, but it will not go away, because it is where most White Americans can still find the revivalism which pervaded the formation of American White culture. That brand of religious enthusiasm is buried in the depths of the psyches of not only the Southern poor, but most of the rest of White America. Whoever would move them from their nostalgia for the unjust systems of the good old days must at least feed and motivate their spirits with a gospel that is culturally familiar. It must stretch the growing edges of their die-hard world view from within, rather than insulting their roots by trying to coerce them with a sterile cult of theological elitism. The militant and idiomatically fluent pastor of an adoring Black congregation is bound to suspect that his prophetic White counterpart gets cast out of his church because his flock are spiritually hungry, more than because they are unalterably opposed to a justice never presented in their language. As Dr. Miles Mark Fisher suggested to me in 1945, when I was already trying to change the South, "Brother Mitchell, don't *use* your influence 'til you *get* it."

For some, this will seem strangely similar not only to a form of cop-out gradualism, but to a complete capitulation, so far as intellectual stimulation and integrity are concerned. I am tempted to do a "high-level" cop-out in response, and defend my insistence on the use of the native language of persons by giving forth a scathing and Ivan-Illich–type of indictment of the vested interests in theological jargon. However, a less elitist, and therefore more appropriate, defense of this semantic insistence is that of making things available to ordinary persons in their own frame of reference. Where that frame needs changing, it cannot be ignored, bypassed, nor destroyed, but it can be stretched to include new perspectives. This is sometimes called hermeneutics, the norm of which is to interpret something from one culture into real meaning and relevance in another. And the best of Black preachers know that everything in Tillich which is worth knowing is capable of translation into the language and living concerns of rather ordinary folk. The challenge is not to the audience so much as to the would-be intellectual translator. This is *true* wisdom and mental integrity, that you *feed* the sheep. Tillich's *Courage to Be* is *food* for Blacks, when understood.

A final challenge to be answered is the one that my advice is too parochially based—that what works with Blacks will not necessarily work elsewhere. Obviously this is true of cultural minutiae, but I am reminded of a mistake I made in connection with this sort of thing some years ago. It was at the height of the death-of-god controversy, and I was, as now, proposing a kind of Black solution to a White theological educator. His answer was that it wouldn't work in his culture because "the symbols are dead." I blurted out a response which I thought at the time was both true and clever. I told him that the preaching he was doing would kill *any*thing, symbols included. I have since discovered that I was neither correct nor clever. God symbols very distinctly are *not dead* in White culture, as already mentioned in the reference to the hymn, "Amazing Grace." The most one can generalize about comparative cultures is that the symbols may be buried deeper among some segments of some cultures, causing a greater problem of retrieval and access. But the great and profound theological concerns of all races and cultures are still the same; and the preaching and teaching which fails to heal the breach between rational and deeply nonrational ultimate concern is woefully inadequate and perhaps arrogantly naive.

Finally I suggest that the seed transconsciously transmitted or planted has a way of living on which goes beyond our fondest hopes. It can dominate a whole culture and perpetuate itself in a wide range of human activities when deep calleth unto deep, and folk have no notion they are witnessing or teaching or planting. A whole world view is implicit in both the gospel and the blues singing of Black culture, and what it says about God is beamed to the least likely and the most unreligious person, formally speaking. This fact was dramatically illustrated to me many years ago, when a Black nurse, head of an obstetrics ward in a Brooklyn hospital, casually reported to me the reactions of mothers from the various cultures. She said that there were general patterns followed by Italian and Jewish and various other mothers. But the one that struck her was that of the Black mothers in labor. Unlike some, who went so far as to curse the husbands who impregnated them, the most "depraved" Black woman reared in Black culture, no matter how divorced from the church—no matter what profanity she used, or what dope, or how much of a prostitute—no matter how she talked previously, would clean up her speech and call on God when the worst labor pains hit her. Whatever else she may have said or done, in the worst crisis, it was "O Lord, have mercy!" A whole culture can, in a sense, be converted and made a friend to grace to help one on to God. And the residue of religion expressed in foxholes is better than none, and a foundation for later growth.

For fear that Black culture might be much weaker in these past twenty-five years, I have recently asked other Black nurses, coast to coast, what they thought of this report. All of them lit right up and suggested that they had never really thought of it before, but now that you mention it, "It's true!" One of them went on to say that she had been a nurse for eighteen years, and she had an amendment to make: "It's not just the women and not just the labor. Let that *real* pain strike one of us, man *or* woman, and we'll call on God no matter what." Whatever the scientific sample, and whatever the possibility that other cultures are equally "primitive" about still calling on God, this much is true; culture at both conscious and "unconscious" levels affects our faith. And the person who would preach with power must speak in the cultural terms which have the power to communicate with every sector of the human consciousness. In this sense, the proclamation of the gospel of Jesus the Christ must be rooted in the culture of the folk.

This insight is not restricted to Black culture. Whether in the Black ghetto, the affluent suburb or the uttermost parts of the earth, the deepest and most meaningful cultural heritage of persons must be identified, respected, and built upon. The greatest weakness of Euro-American Christianity today may very well be the fact that it is unconsciously built on the worst of the fierce paganism of Northern Europe. And this precisely because that folk tradition failed to be recognized and dealt with selectively and purposefully when Europe was claimed for Christ. Certainly one of the greatest strengths of Black Christianity is that it was creatively and adaptively erected on the best of the faith of the African ancestors, as well as the fact that that cultural base was far more humane than Europe's to start with. Preaching that makes meaningful impact on lives has to reach persons at gut level, and it is at this level of communally stored wisdom and cultural affinity that such access to living souls is gained.

3. Preaching as Meaningful Personal Experience

THE MOST important single idea in the previous chapter was that culture-rooted preaching reaches what, for previous want of a better term, we have usually called the *unconscious*. The idea seems neat enough, but it raises the thornier question of precisely *how* culture speaks transconsciously to all sectors of consciousness at the same time. We know very well how to communicate with the "conscious" aspect of persons. We just talk, or rap, or preach. We speak *from* the rational/conscious *to* a rational/conscious. There are no real problems except that it seems to change them so minimally—to do so little good. The hard question is how we participate in the folk culture so as to reach and address personhood in its totality, including the *hidden*-majority aspect of transconsciousness. How does deeper consciousness call unto deeper consciousness?

I want to suggest that the Black preaching tradition has for generations, even centuries, reached these depths intuitively, almost always without the preacher being aware of how or why. I submit that we have been extremely good at it, in fact, and this is why we have maintained a strong, mass-based Black church. We did not throw out either the "baby" of solid content or the "bath" of so-called emotion, which operates in the hidden consciousness. Let us, in the light of these beliefs, rephrase the question. If Blacks have communicated transconsciously more, perhaps, than others, how was access gained to the hidden, elusive, and obstinately autonomous aspects of the Black personality which are mislabeled the *"un*conscious?"

My first response is that this so-called unconscious is formed by *experience* and changed by experience as well. Preaching which would presume to affect this aspect of personhood must seek to change the balance of influential inputs—the data bank of total-person involvements which have, in their own highly logical way, formed the allegedly unconscious patterns of people. The great revolution in communication, which was launched by such seminal minds as Marshall McLuhan's, heralded experience as the key factor. But the spin-off never reached the pulpits of the majority culture and class. However, experience had all along been the rule rather than the exception in the pulpits and pews of the masses of Black America, and this tradition has been sufficiently road-tested in the past two centuries to make it worthy of study as experience-centered preaching and worship.

My second response is that Black preaching has not reached such an *"un*conscious" simply because it is not, in fact, *un*conscious. The word is a misnomer, because the aspect reached is not at all literally unaware. *All* of human consciousness is aware and therefore conscious, but we in the West have erroneously equated consciousness with reason *and* awareness, lightly assuming that the absence of reason automatically means the absence of awareness. Rationality is traditionally assumed to operate only in the visible minority of the floating object we call consciousness. The majority of the object is beneath the surface of the pool and therefore presumably out of reach of normal communication or reason. I would agree that the depths respond more slowly to purely rational processes, but that is because the depths employ a different communications system. This is quite clearly not to say that the depths of consciousness have no law or reason, but that the data employed is for want of better words existential as opposed to abstract.

To be sure not all of Black preaching has measured up to the highly transconscious description I have advanced here, but certainly *some* of it has. It employs, as did the previously mentioned Pastor Marshall of early nineteenth-century Savannah, the cream of both cultures, being *based* on the African. Admittedly, this is not even a majority of contemporary Black preaching, but it is still the growing edge of the liveliest church tradition in American Protestantism; and it is a most promising model. So it deserves serious scrutiny. This analysis is frankly a search for viable models and not a comprehensive critique of Black tradition or the Black churches. It is a searching review of what has been a most creative tradition of preaching, which has at the same time remained relatively and surprisingly unchanged since the early nineteenth century—a one-hundred-fifty-year track record.

My third and technically more specific response to this "how" question is that, generally speaking, the best of Black preaching has communicated not by argument but by art. It has stated that which was logically irrefutable in ways which were artistically and existentially irresistible. Argument and essay deal primarily with the rational conscious. Art and symbol deal with profound truth and logic, while at the same time addressing the totality of transconscious humanity. The art of Black preaching is not *less* than logical; it is logical on *more levels* or wave lengths, addressing both the intellect and the feelings/emotions, the obvious mentality and the subtle mentality called the unconscious by some, but more accurately the intuition and feelings or sensitivities.

In contrast with the essay, artistic speech tends to depend more on vivid and realistic pictures or dramas of truth and symbol and of experience. People comprehend pictorially what they cannot comprehend conceptually. Images well-painted and action well-narrated also provide, so to speak, a video-tape rerun of an experience. Not only does this refresh intellectual memory; it calls forth all the deep feelings which accompanied the original experience, or the original ritual or other retelling of a meaningful story. The root tradition of oratory and graphic and performing arts in Africa served this precise type of communications function—the recall of tradition, the honor of ancestors, and the reinforcement of what they taught.

As opposed to Western art, which is purposefully nonfunctional, African art is never art for art's sake. Nor is it ever elitist, appealing to the intellectually privileged and idle rich. The African art/communication tradition out of which Black preaching comes is communal, with much less distinction between the main performer and the total community. Because of this functionality and absence of art-for-individual-ego, much of Africa's best art has been yielded up to the museums of America and Europe. It was easily obtained, not because it was thought lightly of, but simply because the purpose for which it was created was considered accomplished already. It was considered valuable, but its worth was assumed to have been realized. It is for reasons similar to this that the art of Black preaching has not been widely collected or rigorously defined and analyzed. Once it had portrayed its meaningful images and experiences, the Black sermon had accomplished the purpose for which it was called into being. What else was there to do?

Of course, candidly speaking, the Black preacher has not traditionally thought of his work as art or poetry. He has only been interested in its function. Black preachers easily see as art the highly functional singing of a preacher's daughter named Aretha Franklin, but the great similarities do not suffice to cause them to see themselves as artists. They are trapped in an alien language and a frame of reference which reserve "art" for the elite and popular musical art for the nonserious. It is time we Black preachers broke out of this and saw ourselves as artists in the highest sense, conveying crucial truth not by frontal assault against persons on an exclusively rational battleground, but by the creative weaving of experiences in which the whole person is immersed. (That, incidentally, is not a Baptist commercial.) The goal of Black preaching is to recreate a meaningful experience which communicates transconsciously, nourishing the whole human being. This is indeed high art.

BECOMING A PREACHER-ARTIST

For fear that some will reply that artists are *born,* not made, let me hasten to deal with how one becomes an artistic initiator of meaningful experiences—a transconscious communicator. Belief begets belief, as deep calls unto deep; and our challenge is to free ourselves up as preachers, so that we can communicate on *all* the human wave-lengths, not just the rational conscious. By some definitions, at least, this is all art is. This confronts us, however, with several demanding implications.

First, *one cannot generate a rerun of an experience one has never had personally nor appropriated.* One's depths cannot cry out a message or conviction never lodged in those sacred precincts in the first place. To proclaim truth transconsciously one must possess it likewise, or at gut level. I find myself telling preaching class after preaching class that sermons must come because the depths cry that they have something to say, and not because it's their turn and they have to say *some*thing. In the counseling I consider so essential to the teaching of the art of preaching, I spend hours seeking to find what students believe deeply. It is a waste of time to try to help a person build a sermon about anything that is not deeply his or hers.

One of the tragedies confronted in seeking the belief base for preaching is that in some it is so small and so inaccessible. Modern "intellectual honesty" has inhibited people about facing the fact that they do have deep feelings about some things. In fact, they feel so deeply about some principles that they bet their whole lives on them. And yet they shy away from expressing these beliefs, often even to themselves. My first task is to help a person isolate and define deep feelings, and then to help in giving utterance to these foundational concerns. Once the process is begun, students discover an increasing flow of their own preaching-strength material. And this is done within the limits imposed by their healthy insistence on avoiding outdated pseudoabsolutes. It is so easy because they simply release concerns too long repressed by a false and often unconscious commitment to the sterile wastes of an exclusively rational/scientific world view. No person lives only by what he or she understands rationally or can verify scientifically. In fact one's most important decisions are made without this kind of data, or by faith.

It should come as no surprise that people immersed in the Black Experience should have been forced to keep their belief base a lot nearer the surface and accessible, even though the faith was very deep. This has been evident in the preaching of almost all, including the most trained, formally speaking. The crucible of oppressed existence gives one many experiences with profound meaning, and the tapes of those experiences come in very handy. The inhibitions of academia are a luxury one can ill afford.

But we preach Christ, and the message requires far more tapes from the Bible than from any other source or sources combined. *It is vitally important, therefore, that the artistically transconscious preacher learn the art of telling a Bible story meaningfully.* No single art is nearly so important as this. Where seminaries have enrolled larger numbers of Blacks, the first discipline to feel the impact has been biblical studies. The reason is simple enough. The greatest single element in the genius of Black preaching has been the application of the African oral traditional methods to the biblical oral tradition. In many ways, their treatment of the material, out of their own frame of reference so similar to that of the Old Testament, brings the Bible back to its beginnings, increasing authenticity.

The best of Black Bible story performances, however, require *at least* the same homework levels that everybody else has to engage in. *Very careful study is required to get enough real facts to do an honest work of biblical art in an "eyewitness" account*—a masterpiece of the transconscious communication of a tale, if you please, from the Holy Bible. In the terms already used, one both has some deep experiences of one's own, and one appropriates others, chiefly from the Bible. To gain these for oneself, comprehensive information must be fused with inspired imagination. Then the narrative becomes so much one's own that it can be shared on a deep-unto-deep basis.

Example

One of the best-known beginnings of a Bible story in the whole Black preaching tradition is, "I saw John, down on the Isle of Patmos, early one Lord's Day morning." For some this has become a ludicrous assertion. But it is still possible that it is said with seriousness. Indeed, the preacher-artist *must* say it with a kind of sincerity in order to make of the story a meaningful, literally "eyewitness," account. The fact is that the Black preacher who "saw John" was often telling the poetic truth; he *did* see John. He had read and meditated about it so long that he had an authentically personal witness to give. Only such a witness from the total person can help other total persons to "see John" themselves, and to enter into his perception of the gospel. And when they have *seen* John or Jesus or God the Father, himself, they will never forget the picture nor the person.

The use of vivid imagery out of the transconsciously effective folk tradition does more than communicate in the present. It establishes in the hearer a whole new personal data bank—a person's own collection of tapes of meaningful experiences. The image-message is unforgettable not only because it has been powerfully preached, but because it has been and/or will be reinforced by preached images of equal impressiveness. If the response of some Black audiences to some sermons seems extreme to the outsider, it may be because one cannot know how much meaning the folk-tape preached that Sunday has already accumulated through the years. Conversely, when a Black preacher goes to a congregation of differing culture and predictably finds no response, he will likely conclude that they are spiritually dead. The actual truth may simply be that they all have a different set of tapes. Or, again, they may be spiritually impoverished rather than dead, having grown up in a culture of whatever race in which churches didn't provide people with a collection of tapes of meaningful experiences. No preacher can start by wishing his flock had "the" background. One can and must simply begin, inside the audience's cultural frame of reference, to give them a spiritual tape collection of meaningful experiences.

This reminds me of one of my favorite tales, told by the late E. C. Estell of Dallas. He would explain the failure to elicit response as similar to the effort to get rain in Dallas, after a long drought. The City heard of an aviation company which had precipitated rain over a place in Colorado, and they were hired to cause rain at Dallas. They flew back and forth and they spent thousands of dollars, and nothing happened. The hopeful population watched the skies and there was no question about it. The contract was being fulfilled. But *nothing* happened! Not a drop of moisture came as a result of this massive effort. Dr. Estell asked, "You know why? There wasn't anything up there *to* come down."

The preaching tradition that doesn't systematically store biblical and other tapes of experiences involving great truth and deep feeling will likewise work and work, to no avail. "There won't be anything in them *to* respond." The Black pulpit has to its everlasting credit a rich tradition that people call on and live by and, thank goodness, continue to respond to in the sermon/happening.

However, this data bank of meaningful story/experiences has to be more than a set of well-researched facts in the mind of the preacher. *The story must be internalized in the preacher, peopled by characters he has known for years and for whom he has such deep feelings that he can authentically recreate the action and communicate the experience.* A kind of saturation is required.

A good example of the effectiveness of the story with which the preacher is saturated is the common sermon climax in the Black tradition, concerning the preacher's conversion experience. "I can tell you the day and the hour when my dungeon shook and my chains fell off. I looked at my hands, and my hands looked new. I looked at my feet, and they did too." There follows a deeply moving account of how the preacher was picking cotton or driving a mule or just seeking the Lord, and suddenly he found peace and forgiveness. It was and is so tremendously effective that I used to feel that it was pure emotional manipulation, and as a teenager I resented the power the preacher had when recounting such. I know now that it was contrived at times, but it was much more than that historically, and it is very often much more than that now.

To examine this phenomenon critically yields the immediate insight in this context that the conversion story is the one story the preacher *tells* best because he *knows* it best, with or without any previous preparation. He tells it effectively because he has to do no research or memorization to produce the feeling-laden, graphic details that make for a meaningful experience. It is too bad such preachers are so frequently limited to such a very few stories which they can tell with equal effectiveness. The frequent use may not be a matter of manipulation in the cynical sense; it may be honestly giving the *best* one has.

The conversion story is effective, also, because it has a long history of parallels in other lives. Almost any Black believer has a personal collection of conversion tales or tapes, the most important being one's own. If that was meaningful, they all are; and the preacher who is desperate for impact will understandably tap this reservoir of deep meaning. Here, at least, there is a basis for a dependable if not indeed predictable response.

Still another aspect of the effectiveness of the conversion tale is the fact that the preacher literally takes his own part in the drama. Henry Sloan Coffin of New York's Union Seminary used to warn us against what he called "ecclesiastical nudism," but there is another sense in which preachers must be especially real when they give a personal testimony, however frequently or infrequently that might be. And the problem of portraying other dramatic parts is that of getting "into" them as fully and as easily as one gets into one's own part. Greatness in the Black pulpit almost invariably involves the ability to get into parts, especially biblical parts, with as much ease and impressiveness as one gets into one's own.

This point was brought forcibly home to me some years ago after a lecture I did on Black preaching, at the School of Theology at Claremont. A Black student was even more delighted than I to realize that point after point from my lecture had already been shared with him by his preacher-father. But his warmest and most enthusiastic response concerned a point he had hesitated to share in public. He happened to be an actor, star of a now-terminated television series. With an odd timidity and a kind of surprise, he reported, "You know, what you were saying about being saturated with a story or a part sounds just like what I have to do on the job." We both almost shouted. "That's *exactly* it! Why in the world didn't you share that with the whole group?" No less than any actor, the preacher has to think a part, dream a part, live with it until it has the power to overshadow him, even as the African ancestors overshadow those who play their parts in today's festivals of the living dead. This is just exactly how the African portrayer of the ancestor gets ready to take his part, and this is why the whole community can't forget the traditions. The ancestors actually *live* again! And even though Black preachers have had to internalize a huge repertoire of parts, they have done so with enough effectiveness that in the Black ghetto folks still crowd a church to hear a good sermon. They may have heard the part or the story a hundred times, but every fresh performance, if you please, gives new insights as well as inspiration. The authentically folk-idiom preacher communicates most effectively from his wholeness as a person to the whole person in the folk audience, employing replays of other whole persons which appeal to every sector of the hearer's transconscious.

I propose to offer some guidelines for the folk-culture development of a meaningful experience. But first it would seem important to consider what is meant by the word meaningful. After all, the guidelines should apply to content as well as impact, and nothing has been said to clarify this aspect of the goal of a meaningful experience.

THE MEANING OF "MEANINGFUL"

A stereotypical Western response to what I have said thus far might be that I have said literally nothing about content and everything about communication vehicles. Such is the Euro-American addiction to abstractions and to the dichotomy of form and substance. The utterly uncomplicated response is that *Moses and David and Jeremiah and Jesus are their own content,* as is the case with all oral tradition. *They are living epistles read not alone with the literate eye but with one's whole being.* By identifying with the biblical character and his or her spiritual strengths and struggles and victories the hearer appropriates both the experiential tape and the doctrinal tradition, spelled out in living terms. Black preaching in America is the lineal descendant of an African tradition in which the profoundest meanings have been best expressed artistically for a thousand years. This superiority is evident not only in the Western-style "comprehension" achieved, but in the more important rhetorical goal of *influence on life*—the maintenance of a stable and humane society. In Black, the medium has *always* been the message.

However, while preaching must be done in the people's own living images, all of which have meaning, this alone will not suffice. *Preaching must also relate intentionally to their deepest existential needs as unique persons and groups of persons.* As simple and as obvious as this may sound, the fact is that most preaching in *all* cultures today ignores people's deepest human needs. In listening to a great many sermons, one would get the impression that our deepest need was for a new commentary on the headlines or a few fresh and striking goodies on the human psyche. Yet we all know very well that folks have far more knowledge than they ever use. It is useless except for status purposes because it is lodged in an aspect of consciousness too shallow to reach the whole person, feelings and all. Beyond cute facts, the desperate need is for patterns of life-sustaining meaning, targeted to reach "what's happening" and hurting *now.* The African community, which has long depended on oral communications to interpret the communal life, has traditionally embraced its need-oriented messages quite naturally—rendering them normative without resistance. And this must be the goal of modern gospel proclamation, that persons *see* and *feel* the self-evident truth, *gladly* following where it leads.

In fact, the only way one can judge the success or failure of any pulpit's content or meaning is the effect it has on human behavior—the fruit it bears. The targets or goals are not in books but in people. Whatever the enslaved preacher used to say, it had an awful lot to do with the fact that Blacks didn't die out after all, despite the unbelievable atrocities committed against them. The problem is to keep them from mechanically repeating what met needs a century ago to persons in the context of today's major shifts.

Recently I asked a seminar of preachers what their deepest needs were, as persons rather than preachers. We wrote ten needs on the board. Then I turned around and asked point-blank how many of them had preached a sermon on how many of these topics. The startling response was that one preacher had preached one sermon on perhaps the most pervasive problem of the bunch, and he had used one of the greatest texts in the Old Testament. But that was a score of perhaps one, on a possible scale of ten topics times ten preachers, or one hundred. I cannot overemphasize the fact that most of our needs are at the less-verbalized levels or aspects of awareness, and that intellectually impressive approaches don't reach people's existential concerns about survival and guilt and the meaning of their lives.

There are, of course, fresh insights bordering on new facts which must be included in the old gospel for this new day. But even here the sharing must be transconscious. Nothing new or old is assimilated into the whole personality which is not transmitted on all wave lengths.

I sat one day many years ago in a juvenile hall, chatting with a teenage girl who was very mixed up. Early in her life her grandma had gone a little overboard in some teachings about predestination which she had shared with her. Then her father whom she loved dearly had been killed in an auto accident. Suddenly, Black culture or no Black culture, she developed some deep misconceptions about the justice of God; and she manifested some very antisocial behavior which landed her in jail. My job was to assist her towards a new and sound understanding of the character of God and of all reality. My task was a heap bigger than the reading of a few choice verses about the justice of God and the clever interpretation thereof. My insights were utterly useless until I could tell her on all wave lengths, on a gut-to-gut basis, that I had once been a thief. It began to get through when a former pickpocket of a pastor "ran down" the way God's justice and mercy dealt with him. The new insight came alive when the sound doctrine was warmly and, if you please, artistically symbolized *to* a whole person, *by* a whole person.

Since I have been working on this material and thinking more about real needs, I have found myself disciplined to preach on utterly new topics, so far as my experience was concerned. There was one on if and why the youth of today are lazy. And there was an answer to the troubled question of a lady who wanted to know why children trained up for sure in the way they should go, still don't always follow in it. What does Proverbs 22:6 mean? Then there was an answer to the well-grounded charge of some militant Black nonchurchmen that there are many White materialist subterfuges built into the Black man's celebration of Christmas. Finally there was the recall of the need for a sermon on how to gain patience instead of simply repressing hostility. The term "meaningful" is very closely related to such current need.

My experience is that the minute one announces the intent to offer a word from God's Word on nitty-gritty issues like the ones I have mentioned, the attentive ear of the audience is guaranteed. There is in fact a kind of eager expectation. And at the end there is a most rewarding gratitude. Recently, in a Methodist church in the South, I was greatly helped in preaching by the support of a stewardess in the front pew. Imagine my surprise when this saintly sister shook my hand after and pointedly said, "You lifted my load this morning." She, too had been perplexed by Proverbs 22:6. What greater satisfaction can there be than that of meeting needs at a deep level and having the joy of being made aware of how it helped?

The best Black sermon-happenings have been the ones in which people learned transconsciously something desperately needed—in which the hearer was led to live through a problem, and through the biblical answer and victory as well. However much some may have mistaken it for otherworldliness, the sermon climax that celebrated a victory in heaven when there was no earthly victory in sight was at least a way of surviving with sanity. Our need now is simply to find victories to celebrate that relate to our *present* needs. This is a way of collecting a tape of a valid experience and answers which can be recalled in the time of need, and from which the necessary truth and strength can be drawn to stand in a trying existence. I want to give an example from Black history of a sermon climax which lived through a problem and the victory. But before this closing illustration we must turn to the guidelines I proposed to give for the challenging task of developing in a sermon the meaningful experiences people need to collect to live meaningfully.

SOME GUIDELINES

1. *Give people adequate time to relate transconsciously, or in depth, to every significant idea of meaning presented.*

No message has been accepted meaningfully, with or without a narration/experience, to which one has not responded and related emotionally, or at gut level. Dr. Gardner C. Taylor once informed an impatient me, "Emotions take time. Feelings do not operate on a push-button basis." We know and teach this in marriage counseling; but we must be just as sensitive to the movements of the slow but powerful deep feelings in the intimate process called preaching.

One good insight, well presented, with emotional contact and impact, is far more effective than a minimodel of the *Summa Theologica* with twelve points. If real communication rather than a show of erudition is the goal, one good idea will be a quite satisfying achievement. Only a kind of deep-level egotism at individual and communal-cultural levels could drive people to attempt the awful scope I hear at times in the would-be learned pulpit. I am reminded of a sermon a student preached in a lab I helped to teach. It was on the theme of Christian priorities. After all the other comments, I criticized the sermon on the grounds that it was miserably illustrated. The student defended by repeating his catalogue of illustrations: the cost of the Vietnam War, the total tobacco and liquor sales of the USA, the cost of cosmetics in this country, and the price we pay for rich farmers not to plant, as compared with the total budget for all churches and related agencies, or the total cost of all welfare payments to the needy. It was an impressive list intellectually speaking. But at deeper levels it moved much too fast to go over like anything but a lead balloon. Any *one* item on the list might have been used with much more effect. He could have done a narrative on the blood-curdling things that happen to welfare clients, while a vastly greater budget goes to kill the flower of youth from all the nations involved in a war nobody wanted. But that wouldn't have reached a place where the hearer had any direct control. I would have illustrated the priorities, as I did recently, by doing a countdown in preparation for the Sunday morning launch to church. I projected a scene with mother at the beauty parlor on Saturday, the scrubbing and hair-combing of children; and the uncomfortable clothing, all with dialogue dramatizing parental impatience. Then I asked what the audience thought a kid would have considered important in preparation for worship. After I did it, a twenty-eight-year-old Ph.D. candidate thanked me and frankly admitted that this had changed the course of his life. He had been "hit below the belt," and he was going to reshape his preparation for church attendance altogether. It was the time taken to paint the *picture* of the priorities that made the difference.

Again on the illustration of priorities, I am reminded of a scene some five years ago, when my wife and I attended a funeral near the Oakland Airport. As we rushed away a lady stopped us to report, "I'll never forget that sermon you preached on giving!" I stopped short and thought to myself, "That's the *last* sermon I'd expect anybody to remember for a whole twenty years." I didn't remember it myself, but she quickly refreshed my memory, gushing forth in great detail. The Golden Gate Fields race track had just opened near our home. During a racing series there gathered every evening, a block up the street a host of penniless people trying to beg or borrow bus fare. As I had circulated among the gamblers I had been struck by the fact that I *never* heard anybody regret that he had bet his last penny on a losing horse. What few regrets I heard were to the effect that they wished they had *more* to bet and presumably to lose. The lady had remembered it so well because it had meant so much to her and her husband, and in fact still did. It had helped them to establish priorities, become tithers, and to feel extremely blessed ever since. I shuddered when I thought of the fact that most of my sermons at that time had been illustrated in the manner of the pupil I criticized, by doing quick surveys from Dan to Beersheba, and making only the briefest stops at any one place.

If I seem to belabor this point, it's because I mean to practice what I preach. One last illustration of the whole problem of ensuring time for a theme to sink in is the contrast between Black and White culture in the field of church music. A traditional Protestant hymn may have six or more stanzas, and its lyrics may cover all the cardinal doctrines of the faith. It is utterly ridiculous to assume that such a hymn will ever do much more than overload the memory, even though a particular stanza may be so meaningful as to be unforgettable. On the other hand, a well-known Spiritual says, "Lord, I want to be a Christian," three times in one stanza, adding "In my heart" a total of six times. That's all the stanza says. Which of these think ye does the most to move whole persons nearer the kingdom?

2. *If you have an idea that can't be translated into a story or a picture, don't use it.*

This second guideline has already been quite implicit in the simple fact that the time to sink in, proposed above, was all used to paint pictures and tell stories. It was not used up in argumentation or syllogisms. *One has made sense of anything only when he can engage in a pictorial symbolization of it.* Anything short of this is a verbal repetition without profound, transconscious understanding. There are no "handles" by which another person can relate to it totally, and this probably means that it is not only unclear but irrelevant. However, to insist on symbolic translation is not to suggest that all should be pictures. It is only to insist that all concepts, once stated, be illustrated well.

This guideline will perhaps imply serious, seemingly culture-oriented judgments against traditional theological education. But I suspect that much of the decline (and fall?) of Protestantism in America is traceable to an elitist clergy, trained away from folk communication in the name of academic as opposed to functional excellence. What I propose by way of symbolization makes training no less easy; it simply suggests that it change focus to the professional goal of clarity and impact among the *common* people, who heard Jesus gladly.

Every great truth of the gospel or doctrine of the churches provides some view of the world and its Creator by which persons literally live, and without which they die or simply exist without meaning. It must be well understood that African captives did not survive two and a half centuries in a torture chamber called slavery in a theological vacuum. They maintained existence and sanity only because they brought a world view from Africa which, with Christian adaptations, provided a theological means of coping with a cruelly absurd and impossible condition. They wrote no creeds, but they expressed profound Christian folk belief in song and tale and shout and, until pressured away from it, dance. They had done this for centuries before, and the most moving corpus of material I know of on the providence of God is in West African proverbs. No better set of images to illustrate Paul's statement about God working things together for good (Rom. 8:28) exists than the collection of African poetic proverb-pictures. The faith of Christians blended with and mutually enriched Black belief, but the crucial convictions remained in the image medium. The functionality for human survival of this graphic way of *seeing* religious truth transconsciously, rather than handling it only verbally, has been established. A new kind of intellectual respectability is now being added, since *image iteracy* is rapidly replacing traditional Western word-orientation everywhere.

When an enslaved African saw the transcendence and glory

and majesty of God it was no mere vision, detached from real life. It had deep, immediate significance. The theological implications of the Spiritual "My God Is So High" were profound, but they dealt serious blows to slavemasters who thought themselves gods over slaves. When the figure was decoded, the real significance was that *masters* could not circumvent God—"You can't git over Him" nor under, nor around. In the same song it was clear that Blacks had no intentions of trying to circumvent God, for they had walked and talked with him. "One day as I was walking . . . my Saviour spoke unto me." The so-high God was not inaccessible, they discovered, but his transcendence was a firm limit to what they had to fear in a master.

A similar guarantee was implied in the theology of the Spiritual "He's Got the Whole World in His Hand." How much more expressive than a theoretical statement of the "omnipotence of God!" Yet that is what it meant, and slave life was bearable so long as there was enough faith to know that an all-powerful and just God would some way make it all make sense. Even the currently unfashionable notion of the judgment of God still appeals to me, as it did to my enslaved foreparents, because I see too much injustice here for it all to be squared up on this side of Jordan. In this sense, the hell taught to African captives to scare them into compliance actually backfired. It was a new idea, but it fitted into their adamant affirmation of life by explaining how God would square it all up, in due season.

Theology and ethics and anything else worth preaching may and perhaps must be stated in careful argument. But it won't reach the whole person until it is translated into moving and graphic art and symbol—word pictures and narrations.

3. *The painting of graphic pictures and the narration of moving experiences requires abundant, realistic detail.*

For instance, most biblical accounts are similar to dried milk. The major substance is there, but it is not palatable until it has been reconstituted with the addition of an ordinary thing like water. In the reconstitution of the Bible story, the "ordinary" is the details of life which were so commonplace that the recorder took them for granted. They fell out of the written account and eventually out of memory. The Bible storyteller today can reclaim them only by careful study of history, archeology, ancient society, and language. To these one must add the exegetical and expositional assistance of scholars and an inspired imagination, where still more details are necessary to an "eyewitness" account.

Once this kind of homework has been done, the preacher can then begin to move into the scenes and "learn the parts" and the action that have been generated for the drama. I want to give at least a brief example of what I mean here, although it will be fleshed out in later chapters. It comes from a sermon literally written by a preaching class which I supplied with a text and theme and challenged to do an outline. The text was Paul's word to the Philippians about thinking "on these things," such as the just and the good reports, if there be any virtues at all to be thought of (Phil. 4:8). The theme or key idea was from my research in slave narratives. I was convinced that African captives didn't go crazy because, despite the vast majority of cruel suffering in their lives, they focused consciousness on their few blessings. They took the initiative to choose their internal living space. With a genius for psychic survival, if there was *any* praise, they thought on these things.

A White student suggested to the class that Paul was an excellent example of this same phenomenon referred to as a kind of positive thinking plus. So instead of a long theological exegesis of the text, he argued for a character study of the person who wrote it and illustrated it superbly with his own life. He suggested that because of such a positive attitude, Paul could be as productive as a prisoner as anywhere else. When he was chained to a guard, the question could well be asked as to who was the guard and who was the detained. In an unexpected and extemporaneous rendition of the sermon which I happened to do, I was able to follow class directions because I had quite a few "tapes" of Paul. There were lines like these:

good
Illus

When under arrest Paul didn't sit in sorrow and cry, "I don't know why I have to suffer this disgrace. Is this what I get for trying to serve the Lord?" No! He looked around for a pen and some paper and wrote words of scripture that might never have been in the Bible otherwise.

And when he got tired of writin', I can see him as he looked at the soldier on the other end of the chain and said, "Lookee here! I got me an audience. And he can't get away. I believe I'll try a little gospel on him. And if he gets a little sleepy, I'll shake the chain." For Paul the *chain* held the *soldier,* and in his mind *Paul* was *free.* Why? Because whatsoever was good about that situation, he thought on *these* things.

The sermon went on to show how slaves did the same, and how their mind set could make one wonder who was the master, and who was the slave. As is still true of Blacks in America, slaves praised God immeasurably more than the ruling class. Such living illustrations explicate the subtleties of the text and of Black experience far more effectively, and the little details are the lifeblood of the meaningful narrative.

Of course, living details are not the sole tool of meaningful speech used in the Black tradition. Striking speech forms and rhetorical devices such as aphorisms have long been popular both in Africa and America. Dr. Martin Luther King, Jr., illustrated this quite well. But even in the African oratorical tradition the main goal was to use the inherent power of images rather than of arguments. No matter how colorful and even at times ornate the speech, the intent was to sway the hearer with language that reached feelings as well as their rational counterpart in the obvious-conscious.

Still another guideline from the Black preaching tradition has to do with timing and climax. But that is so large a topic that I shall deal with it at greater length later, in the chapter on "Preaching as Celebration." The final guideline to be considered now has to do with process, or the style of preparation that goes with the style of preaching proposed. How do you produce one or two works of art, each replete with meaningful experiences, every week? Failure to address this difficult question would repeat one of the commonest errors of the pulpit, the error of questions and criticisms, with no answers and positive instruction to match. Yet to give details runs the risk of seeming to put revelation on a Western, assembly-line basis. Here, rather, is a set of disciplined circumstances in which revelation and creation may more readily take place.

4. *In order to prepare sermons which include elements of authentic art, with power to generate meaningful experiences, the <u>raw materials must be in hand, ready for unhurried creativity</u>, as soon as possible.*

Preachers simply must stop the practice of sitting at a desk and pleading for power to be breathed into human homework completed as recently as 11:30 P.M., Saturday. The Black preacher, whose neighborhood image has long included a too leisurely if not outright lazy aspect, has often been doing much more than the fishing or hunting or rocking in a chair that appeared on the surface. Out of the visual reach of critical observers he has been creating stories and painting pictures, processes which cannot be completed on a stop-watch basis. Today's preacher of every culture is far busier than the "leisurely" Black parson of the rural South, but the guideline still prevails. And those who have not already found ways to be creative on the run may find the following emergent tradition to be of some assistance.

The homework required to develop the details mentioned in the last guideline simply must be done early. At the latest this would be the Monday preceding the Sunday when a sermon is to be preached, unless the preacher has an inexhaustible collection of tapes of character and other details already stored, over a long period of years, in a vivid memory. After all the reading possible, it takes *time* to develop the common details that transform the words back into living accounts. <u>The best of reading, in other words, will only beget mechanical repetition unless the material has had ample time to "soak in" and</u> generate a lifelike personal vision of what happened.

During my own years as a pastor responsible for two sermons per week, I called the process following the reading and research "putting it on the back burner to simmer." The hard data available was essential to honest proclamation, but the preacher had to have time unhurriedly to think and live his way into the text or related narratives, as well as nonbiblical narrative illustrations, and into all the characters contained therein. They need time to become familiar friends, present already to the preacher in every aspect of consciousness, if they are to be projected to the hearer's total personhood.

Once this accurate information is in hand, the modern preacher/pastor makes his busy rounds, using every possible opportunity to look on the "back burner" and stir up the exegetical and other data cooking there. The elements of the sermon rise to consciousness as the pastor drives from place to place, or eats alone, or relaxes in a waiting room, or tries to go to sleep or to wake up. All the while the preacher is getting into character as an eyewitness or participant, and the characters take on flesh and blood in the process of constant companionship. The seemingly petty but creative and powerful configurations of details that emerge from this meditation on the move are faithfully recorded on an ever-present scratch pad, to conserve whatever God and a good imagination may yield. When Sunday comes, preaching is still done in awe and trembling, but it is not overly difficult to produce the meaningful images and narratives which have been used through the years to move mankind and to stimulate a saving and empowering faith.

I never cease to be amazed at the powers of the laity to recall the meaningful experience of a good story or picture with accuracy and often with deep and appropriate feeling. The Black tradition includes a congregation which answers back, but it includes an interior response that lasts through the years. Slave narratives collected in 1936 retain fantastic details from sermons heard sixty to seventy or more years earlier. One of the most relevant and creative presentations of the gospel I ever heard came to me in this way. I conclude this chapter with a reconstituted *rendering* of Ned Walker's account, given in South Carolina in 1936, as I think and feel my way into it.

Now 'bout Uncle Wash's funeral. You know Uncle Wash was the blacksmith in the fork of the road, across the railroad from Concord Church. He had been a mighty powerful man. He used the hammer and the tongs on behalf of *all* the people for miles and miles around.

Uncle Wash joined the Springvale A.M.E. Church, but he kinda fell from grace, I guess. Somehow he was 'cused of stealing Marse Walter Brice's pig, and I guess he was guilty. At any rate, he was convicted and sent to the penitentiary. While he was down there he contracted consumption and had to come home. His chest was all sunk in, and his ribs was full of rheumatism. He soon went to bed and died. He was buried on top of the hill, in the pines just north of Woodward.

Uncle Pompey preached the funeral. Lots of White folks was there. Marse William was there, and so was his nephew, the attorney general from Arizona. The biggest of the crowd was our folks, and Uncle Pompey really knowed how to preach a funeral. I never will forget that one.

Uncle Pompey took his text from that place in the Bible where Paul and Silas was a-layin' in jail. He dwelt on Uncle Wash's life of hard work and bravery—how be tackled kickin' horses and mules, so's crops could be cultivated and harvested and hauled. He talked about how he sharpened dull plow points, to make the corn and cotton grow, to feed the hungry and clothe the naked. He told what a good-hearted man Uncle Wash was, and then he allowed as how his goin' to jail didn't necessarily mean he didn't go to heaven. He declared it wasn't eternally against a church member to get put in jail. If it hadda been, Paul and Silas wouldn't 'a made it to heaven, and he knowed *they was there. In fact, they was a lot* of people in heaven what had been arrested. Then he went to talkin' 'bout a vision of Jacob's ladder.

"I see Jacob's ladder. An' I see Brother Wash. He's *climbin'* Jacob's ladder. Looks like he's half way up. I want you all to pray with me that he enter the pearly gates, Brothers and Sisters. He's still a-climbin'. I see the pearly gates. They is swingin' open. An' I see Brother Wash. He done reached the topmost round of the ladder.

Let us sing with all our hearts that blessed hymn, 'There is a fountain filled with blood.' "

When they sang the second verse, 'bout "The dyin' thief rejoiced to see that fountain in his day," Uncle Pompey cried out over the crowd, "I see Brother Wash as he enters in, and that dyin' thief is there to welcome him in. Thank God! Thank God! He's made it into paradise. His sins has been washed away, and he has landed safe forever more."

I don't need to tell you that the women started to shout on the first verse, and when they got to singing about the dyin' thief bein' in heaven, and they seen the 'surance of grace that was in it, they like to never quit praisin' God.[1]

4. Preaching as Celebration

Praise it Lord!

THE BEST of gospel preaching is at once proclamation and celebration. Let us agree then as to what we mean by the term celebration. For our purposes celebration is both the literal and the symbolic or ritual expression of praise or joy. It may be in regard to an event or a person, historical or legendary, past or present; or it may relate to an object or a belief. A part of the genius of Black preaching has been its capacity to generate this very kind of celebration, despite the hardest of circumstances. This genius for celebration is partly responsible for the fact that enslaved and otherwise oppressed Blacks have survived the seemingly unbearable. When the oppressor thought they were too ignorant or insensitive to pain to know the depth of their plight, they were in fact well aware of it, but also involved in a vital tradition which literally sustained them by engaging them in praise of God—the dramatic expression of a world view affirming Creation and Creator and the ineradicable value of the gift of life.

Preaching *without* celebration is a de facto denial of the good news, in *any* culture. Stated positively, what I propose is that preaching *with* celebration greatly enhances the transconscious retention and the true understanding and application of the gospel. It is my purpose here to spell out the meaning and the supporting rationale of these perhaps sweeping statements.

As I have already indicated in the second chapter, the African folk/oral tradition was so accurately communicated from generation unto generation because of rites which were celebrative. The massive corpus was inculcated in the minds of the young under circumstances which were joyous for the most part. That is to say, most of the folk gatherings were around the happy themes of birth, marriage, planting, harvest, and the advancement of the young through the stages of life. Even the feasts about death were not without joy. The result was a well-remembered corpus of proverbs and rites, with many ordinary folk capable of meticulous recall. More importantly, this tradition was so impressed upon the total transconscious that the life decisions of folk were heavily conditioned if not absolutely controlled by traditional belief. The importance of celebration in this cultural forebear of the Black religious tradition is inescapable. The joy and celebration which characterize Black worship even now are very important in the explanation of miraculous survival of this beauty and richness under the shadows of the oppressed ghetto.

Lest somebody get the notion that this is just the tenacity of a traditional "trip" of Black folks, let us look at the role or function of joy, fun, ecstasy, or celebration in worship, particularly preaching. In the first place, that which is joyously given, received, and celebrated is well nigh unforgettable. The emotional/intellectual tape or script is well cut by the etching agent of ecstasy. The transconscious data bank of the soul can much more readily be depended upon to recall that which was recorded in the midst of such pleasant associations. And when in the dark night of the soul it seems impossible to recapture the joy of the celebration, there is a higher signal which may draw it forth from the data pool even so. The first function of celebration in preaching is reinforcement for retention and availability.

The very title of George Leonard's book, *Education and Ecstasy,* indicates how important joy is to real learning even in the public schools. That importance is still greater in the learning of spiritual values and foundations. In a volume entitled *How Churches Teach* I once declared:

> Shouting may, at times, be put on or manipulated. But at its best it *teaches* "Aunt Jane" and all the rest that the presence of God is sheer ecstasy—that before God we can be absolutely free and uninhibited—and that God freely accepts and loves the real person that we have to hide almost everywhere else. The ecstasy of being somebody-to-the hilt for even five minutes, *teaches* enough faith to keep an oppressed and despised Black man courageous and creative for another week.

Ecstasy teaches *and* reinforces teaching. It does not always express itself in shouting in Black tradition, but it does always involve deep feelings. Such feelings generate deep trust levels and inscribe the faith indelibly on the transconscious.

A second function of celebration is its fulfillment and affirmation of personhood and identity by means of free expression, which is accepted in the religiocultural context. This has been mentioned already in the quote above, where the shouting Christian is accepted by God while expressing his or her real feelings. This acceptance by God is mediated by the congregation, whose cultural expectations place high value on the shouting evidence of the presence of the Holy Spirit. If the congregation were to view shouting in a different light, it would be hard to sense the acceptance of God counterculturally. Celebration, therefore, provides a supportive structure in which persons are free to pour forth their deepest feelings and to celebrate their own personhood in the midst of celebrating the goodness of God.

Some time ago I was crushed in an Amanuel Day crowd of thousands, stretched as far as eye could see in all directions from Amanuel Church in Addis Ababa. They were celebrating Ethiopian Orthodox Christmas Eve. As the procession bearing the symbolic Ark of the Covenant passed round and round the church, shouts of great joy arose from wave after wave in a sea of literally happy faces. They were a terribly poverty-striken lot for the most part, and Marx would have called this joy an opiate of the people. But I know that the religious forefathers of these same folk have survived the onslaughts of European and Arab invasion time and again. In the barren wastes to which they have had to retreat to live, they have survived more by an abundance of spiritual feast days than of physical food. Amanuel Day is only one of the nine *minor* feasts, but those thousands were gathered because their chants and cheers, their waving and dancing had meaning there which gave *them* meaning and fulfillment also. The owners of those voices and hands and feet were affirmed as persons while praising God, despite the vastness of their numbers and their great physical need by American standards.

This vast crowd also illustrates a third function of celebration, that of drawing people into community. Celebration is best achieved in the group relationship. It is good, of course, to praise God in solitude, but the enjoyment of God's goodness is multiplied by the sharing of the news. It binds together the host of those who affirm the goodness of God, who are affirmed in his praise, and who joyously affirm others as recipients of that same goodness. The celebrating community may not be personally acquainted, but the group tradition nevertheless provides a supportive context for the expression of the most personal feelings. In turn, the free expression binds the ritual congregation into a warm and emotionally permissive symbolic community.

A fourth facet or function of celebration is that of defining a habitable "living space"—the establishment of a celebrative island of consciousness in an ocean of oppression and deprivation. It might be thought of as roughly equivalent to the Western concept of the power of positive thinking. But it is far more than a wishful and naive attempt to exercise some fancied power of mind over matter. Rather, it couples a realistic facing of the hardest aspects of existence with a firm determination to fix consciousness on whatsoever things exist for which there can be praise to God. The Spiritual puts it, "Nobody knows the trouble I see, Glory Hallelujah!"

Preaching which authentically celebrates the goodness of God and of life provides not only ideas but total experiences for the recall of the hearer. The celebration event as event and not just as comforting thought may then be "rerun" by the person in the oppressed audience, as a means of transcending the discouragement of later circumstances. In so doing one elects to live amidst and to focus consciousness on the joyous elements in past experience, as opposed to the perhaps vast majority of painful elements—the horror story of which one is the chief character and which one is, for the time, powerless to change. A Spiritual expressed the process of focus of consciousness thus: "Woke up this mornin' with my mind stayed on Jesus, Hallelu, Hallelu, Hallelujah!" Preaching which celebrates the goodness of God equips hearers to stay their minds and focus their consciousness, choosing their living space and transcending the tragedies of oppressed existence.

The final role of celebration is that fitting climax to a balanced proclamation which has already included exegesis, exposition, explanation, application, and deeply meaningful illustration. The gospel should have been proclaimed throughout with joy. But the best reinforcement and the greatest expression of joy must naturally occur when, so to speak, the lesson is completed and summarized, and thanks and celebration are offered for it at the end. All else leads up to this climactic moment, and whatever follows is inevitably anti-climax. Like a symphony, the theme is stated majestically and powerfully, with prior elaborations now taken for granted. Fresh spiritual insight and illumination, joyous recall, and persons fulfilled in community are celebrated together.

To take all these blessings for granted to the extent of a bland and unenthusiastic response would be to give evidence of having failed to appreciate and benefit from it in the first place. No blessing is ever enjoyed fully unless and until it is carried from the stage of mere mention to the stage of grateful praise and celebration. The intensity of the celebration is the accurate index to the depth of the response. If in fact the gospel is what we have been saying it is—the power of God unto the very salvation of persons—how can preacher or people respond other than in celebration?

The question that haunts all of us is simply how one goes about the task of preaching in such a way as to make possible the gift of authentic celebration from time to time, especially as we near the close of the proclamation.

The first and most penetrating answer to this hard question is that great celebration is only generated by the treatment of great themes. It should be obvious enough that clever intellectual technicalities do not beget great joy among any save their inventors. And even they can't live by their own noodle nuggets in the storms and crises of life. Black Americans have come through trials and tribulations of suicidal proportions, and they have kept on living when others would have given up long since, simply because they have been fed on the great themes of the culture. These would include the goodness of life in the context of a good creation, and the justice, mercy, goodness and providence of the Creator. These have generated celebration by building a world view among churched and unchurched which upheld a hazardous existence by means of a transconscious trust. Without such high trust and meaning levels, life would have been squandered in a struggle for a security which is otherwise impossible for Blacks in this country and within the gift of God alone. With the embrace of the affirmations of the faith and culture, life is free to be abundant, enjoyed, and therefore celebrated, no matter how brutally beset. Great themes and affirmations beget celebration.

It should be equally obvious that celebration is generated by the satisfaction of deep-seated human needs. Gratitude begets celebration, and gratitude flows naturally when the cry of persons has been heard answered from the Word of God. This may sound trite or old-fashioned, but it is no small thing when a saintly sister says to the preacher, "Son, you lifted my burden this morning." Such a response is heard all too seldom, because it is so infrequently deserved. The comforts of an automated age have not spread to the *souls* of our parishes. Indeed, the saints we serve are more and more isolated and alienated in the midst of their earthly toys. The suburban people-trap also breeds great spiritual needs. With physical existence so well cared for, there is less and less to divert attention from the pressing claims of the ultimate concerns. Persons are more restless than ever until they gratefully find their rest in the God of the great gospel. It is then altogether appropriate that they should celebrate.

Thirdly, celebration is generated by the fulfillment of persons. In the culture of the Black masses this is joyously accomplished in the dialogic character of the preaching tradition. When a Black preacher says, "Surely, this was the Son of God," or "Surely goodness and mercy shall follow me all the days of my life," he pauses after the "Surely." At that point, all who wish may lend a hand in the proclamation of the certitude by offering their own "Surely's." Or when the preacher cries "Have mercy!" in prayer or sermon, he waits for whosoever will to echo the plaintive and ubiquitous petition. Early morning has ancient importance in Black culture, and when the preacher says that Mary went early or "soon" Easter morning, to the tomb, he places the "early" first in the sentence. Then he pauses for the response—the joyous and predictable participation of persons caught up in a story which they literally help to tell.

We shall attempt to spell out later what this says to a dominant culture which has few if any such cultural patterns and expectations of congregational participation. I am quite certain, however, that it does *not* say "Go thou and do exactly likewise." It does not suggest, either, that Whites should rush to their drawing boards and dream up some strange and new experiment in lay involvement in worship, to try to parallel the healthy tradition of Black participation. Perhaps it does suggest that White Protestants in America should look more seriously at their own deep roots, wherein lie a few "Amens" and similar audible responses. It is possible, also, that highly structured liturgical worship should look again at its responses, which could be warmed up a bit to say the least. Whatever emerges in response to the challenging model of Black worship, I am sure that *nourishing truth and personal fulfillment are not truly celebrated in dull silence,* and that all celebration requires participation by all the celebrants.

My final suggestions as to how to foster authentic celebration in preaching have to do with the sensitive timing of the truths presented, coupled with an adequate medium for summation and celebration. For many this may seem an altogether new consideration in organizing a sermon, but timing seriously affects sequence towards celebration. We usually think of sequence in logical, theological, or even chronological terms, but we seldom think of the timing of impact. What is this timing all about? What has it to do with cogency and power?

By timing we really mean emotional pace. To consider timing is to apply and to take seriously the fact that the gospel must be communicated to the whole person, or transconsciously. This takes time, as we have already seen, but time for truth to "sink in" and reach the deeper, slower moving emotions may not be used indiscriminately. Concern for timing involves the weighing of emotional impact. This input, in turn, is used alongside the various other logics possible in the final determination of the sequence of material. It is, of course, understood that the gospel must make a certain kind of sense, but it must do it trans-consciously. Like such other art forms as the symphony, the sermon must avoid erratic movement, emotionally speaking, and it must build up to the final statement/celebration and coda.

There are two obvious extremes in this regard. One is the common practice of utter unawareness of emotional impact. It is the sin of being both overly intellectual and inadequately sensitive to the movements of the feelings of the audience. The other extreme is that of the so-called emotional preacher, whose solid content is conveyed unaware if at all. His chief conscious concern is to move people; and his sole criterion for the little organization he does of his material is that of how it will "slay" the congregation.

In between there is a synthesis which teaches as it moves persons, and moves persons as it teaches. It is my deep conviction that God in his providence will never place his messenger in the predicament of having to choose between the two. In fact, I *know* that he calls on us at all times both to illumine and to inspire. There can never be true learning and growth without deep involvement of the feelings, nor can there be depth of Christian emotion without real growth. Our challenge as preachers is to be as aware of the one factor as of the other, and to build up to a celebration which is, at one and the same time, appropriately summary and reinforcing, as well as unforgettably satisfying emotionally.

Let me share with you a typical problem in timing. One day I was working on a sermon on patience. My research had yielded the usual three points or elements for the body of the sermon, each contributing to the patience in persons. The question was about which point was to come first and which second in the presentation. I toyed with the possibilities of first inductive then deductive reasoning, and I looked for a while at which aspect was prior in the development of the human psyche. I also theorized a bit concerning the doctrinal and/or logical sequence and some practical applications of the doctrines in the actual salvation of persons. The definitive choice was made when I asked myself which point had the message with the highest impact—particularly the illustrations and narratives with the most vivid and gripping material. This choice provided, at the same time, the most natural lead into the highly celebrative portion of the text, a section which I had already easily seen to be best suited for summary and celebration. The specifics sounded about like this.

The item about forgiveness and self-acceptance was lowest on my Richter Scale simply because my illustrations of it were least graphic. The decision could also be supported as first in logical sequence, but matters so deep are not subject to compartmentalization. The chicken-or-the-egg problem of priority was at work, and it was perfectly legitimate to make the decision on the basis of presentation impact. I felt no need to argue with myself about consciously avoiding bad sequence by placing my weakest impact first, even though there were two other grounds on which I might have given the choice a sort of intellectual justification.

The item about the love, acceptance, and understanding of others came second because it seemed to fall there on all counts, including the likely impressiveness of the material to be used as illustration. There was no hint of violence to the other concerns for sequence. But I would hasten to add that most abstract bases for sequence are not that essential to deep understanding. The *emotional coherence* may, after all, make it all hang together far better and more lastingly than any other.

Then came patience as the result of faith in the dominion of God and the direction he has given history. On some sort of deductive basis it might have been first, but it came last in a sequence designed to fit the inductive approach. It also came last from the way it related climactically to the text, as well as from the theme and illustrative material on hand. The inductive-deductive typology was in fact irrelevant, since the faith of such a God-governed world view applies to and undergirds all other elements. This point has still another cultural reason for coming last. It was and is a theme of great importance and response in the Black Experience and the tradition of Black preaching. I dare not suggest that this kind of planning *guarantees* the unusual blessing of God on the effort, but I can at least say that it helps greatly to deal honestly with these factors of impact and its timing.

May I suggest several important guidelines in this regard. For instance, whatever one has of vital and creative new insights should be given relatively early in the message, and subsequently developed and illustrated to a point of acceptance and emotional involvement. Then it may be celebrated. Startling or dazzling fresh perspectives are most essential to good preaching, but they should not be freshly projected in the sermonic climax. The profound understandings which require professional preparation are sure to stretch awareness and sensitivity, and therefore to cause pain. It has been said that where there are no resistance and other attempts to avoid pain, there is no real growth. But few people, if indeed any other than masochists, are able to hurt and celebrate at the same time. The smarting of wounded pride has to begin to die down or disappear, and jarring new demands have to have had time to settle before people can be thankful at all. In other words, the first guideline for the timing of celebration in the climax is that no *new* ideas should be introduced there. No matter how clever, the *surprise* ending cannot have time for adequate transconscious treatment. Climax is the time to summarize, reinforce, and celebrate *previous* illumination.

This implies, also, that celebration should center around the theme and substance of the sermon. This is another way of saying that authentic climax can*not* come from the use of unrelated material which the preacher has found to be very effective in climax. As I have said already many times and places, one of the cardinal sins of Black preachers is that they "have all too often found themselves in the predicament of serving a beef dinner and then drowning the beef in chicken gravy."[1] This tends to diminish if not destroy the impact of the main message by "upstaging" it with ecstasy that is both unrelated and inescapably more memorable. Authentic climactic celebration must stem from an artistic and impressive distillate of the substance of the foregoing message.

Then climactic utterance should be especially characterized by celebrative feelings matching the ideas. That is, the importance of the theme should be expressed in unashamedly moving style and language appropriate to the theme. Whether the climax material is a personal testimony, a relevant Bible story, or an experience of other persons, past or present, it must freely and sincerely employ poetic statement, peroration, and any other rhetorical tool which contributes to the moment of supreme transconscious illumination and inspiration. The "Dream" of Martin Luther King, Jr., would never have become the crucial and classical history that it is had he not dared to pull out all the rhetorical stops of Black tradition, as opposed to modern White pulpit practice. He undoubtedly knew that only such style and language could be appropriate to the task. If the term *soul* applies to Blacks at all, it is especially applicable to the fusion of high content and deep feeling so familiar in the concluding crescendo of the Black sermon.

I want to conclude this treatment of preaching as celebration with some illustrated ideas about how one identifies material appropriate to climactic utterance. However, before doing so let me anticipate a common fear regarding emotional involvement at the celebrative level. It is well expressed in the criticism directed at me some years ago by a Black theological student, just after I had addressed or preached to a large convocation on the Black Church, at the Boston University School of Theology. What he said, in effect, was, "That's very effective oratory, and you really ring the changes right up to a great climax. But it makes me ill, because it reminds me so much of the crowd-pleasing emotional manipulations of a certain Southern governor and candidate for President." I would still plead innocent of any important similarity, but his message was very clear. High impact preaching moves people greatly and is therefore easily capable of abuse. So far as he was concerned it was downright dangerous. He had obviously seen it abused already. And so have I.

All anybody can say in response is that it would be silly to do away with dynamite just because some people use it improperly. With dynamite as well as dynamic preaching the important thing is to follow the instructions of the maker, using the potential only for the purposes prescribed. Just in case there are questions as to what these purposes are, let me briefly restate five guidelines I have already given which I believe strongly to be in keeping with the Maker's purposes:

1. Major in the great themes of the scriptures. They are less amenable to the uses of manipulation.
2. Answer people's deep and real needs, avoiding the temptation to tickle their fancy.
3. Work toward participation by the people. Seriously engage congregations in the acts of celebration, rather than treating them as audience objects to be entertained and thus manipulated.
4. Carefully time the nourishing news so as to facilitate focus and build to celebration of the gospel. Don't get carried away on the first subclimax and go so high there is nowhere higher to go later. The manipulation most

frequent in my observation has been motivated by desperation born of bad timing—early extremes of intensity and no additional possibilities for climactic celebration. If all else is scaled to fit under the peak of proclamation, there is no need to fear a fizzle, nor any cause to resort to manipulative tricks to achieve higher levels of celebration.

5. Then stick scrupulously to the point right through to the last sentence. Manipulative introduction of irrelevant material is the surest sign that the preacher is ill prepared to celebrate on the ground covered. Or it may mean that the material covered did not justify real celebration. All too often have I seen preachers who felt they had to teach a lesson of some sort and then, in conformity to the culture, achieve celebration regardless of how far away they had to reach. Thus were they tempted to drag in the conversion story or a deathbed scene, or a vivid crucifixion. The best and most moving of stories must still be related to the summary, or the celebration destroys the substance. This indeed is manipulation.

As I think of this unvarnished need for and use of rhetorical resources, and of the possible abuses, I am also reminded of a complaint I once expressed to the seemingly inept prosecutor in a murder trial where my only sister had been the victim. The defense had been far more impressive, and I resented the contrast. The district attorney quietly informed me, "When you're trying to take a man's life, you do it with cold and unembellished facts. On the other hand, the defense can virtually do no wrong, so long as his purpose is to save a life." This lifesaving license to use rhetoric to manipulate the jury and confuse justice turned me against capital punishment then and there. But it has since slowly dawned on me also that dramatic intensity may indeed be greatly justified to save a life, both here and hereafter. Power of speech is an evil only when devoted to evil purposes. Suppose a Shakespeare had been inhibited about the use of nonconversational language to express his profound insight!

6. And now may I suggest one additional but not-at-all-original caution about the temptation to be manipulative in the exercise of the power to generate authentic celebration. The preacher who would ask God to confer on his or her feeble utterance the charismatic gift of climactic celebration must diminish or hide self, and be possessed by the message and its Giver. This has been true since the primitive beginnings of Christianity, when the Holy Spirit used men like Peter and Paul. There is a parallel rule of spirit possession which seems to prevail through the traditional religions of West Africa. No man dare use such power or play with it as his own. He who stands *between* God and the seeking eyes of the congregation can only be a thief and a robber. Henry Coffin indelibly impressed on the classes he taught the biblical demand of the contemporary worshiper: "Sir, we would see Jesus."

Let us now conclude with some discussion of criteria for the selection of material appropriate to climax, and some illustrations or examples. It must be understood, of course, that these suggested criteria do not come with the slightest implication of a guarantee of celebration. I only offer hints as to how we may offer to God a more likely worship context in which his *Spirit* may give the supreme celebrative experience. Jesus used the figure of the wind to declare the unpredictability of God's Spirit (John 3:8). What I am suggesting is that we can discover some attitudes and instruments of communication through which the winds of God's Spirit may blow more readily than through others.

First of all, celebration requires positive affirmation. Cheap criticism and clever negativity are often quite effective in arousing audience feelings. Verbal crucifixions can bring people to their feet. But not all deep feeling is celebrative; certainly anger is not. I have already mentioned my quip about fiery utterance, characterizing many White radio pulpiteers as "fiery *mad*," while Black-culture preachers tend to be "fiery glad."[1] The point is simply that a negative gospel is never cause for celebration, except in the sense that one's judgmental declarations are a celebration of sick self-righteousness. Negative comment or prophetic criticism is, of course, essential at some point in virtually every sermon, but the word must conclude on a positive note. Celebration must be based on affirmation! The richness of celebration in the Black tradition is largely traceable to its emphasis on affirmation which covers all of life and creation, and its Creator. The modern preacher who habitually "comes home" or concludes on, "We must . . ." needs to take a lesson from the Black preacher of old whose sermons soared in on such certainty as "God are good!"

Affirmation must be symbolic as well as direct. That which is ordinary must be lifted up symbolically in celebration. Both in African traditional celebrations and in the festivals of the Hebrew-Christian tradition, the concrete focus of the festivity has been a yam, or some wheat, or an ordinary booth or symbolic shanty. Whatever the ultimate meanings, they must be attached to and embodied in that which can be grasped. The Jew and the Black man plagued with injustice cannot celebrate a philosophical treatise on the problem of evil. But they can gain a firm and realistic grip on their oppressed condition and on the joys still to be celebrated when you say it thus:

> Thou preparest a table before me (just an ordinary table) in the presence of mine enemies: thou anointest my head with oil; my cup runneth over. *Surely* goodness and mercy shall follow me all the days of my life: and I will dwell in the house of the Lord forever (Psalm 23:5–6).

The third and next criterion for celebrative material has already been summed up when it was suggested that the language must be appropriate to the theme, employing poetic statement and the like. This does not automatically mean rhetorical adornment, although it often appears so. What it really means is that the language must be capable of expressing deep feeling as well as profound meaning. Because such sentiments are usually avoided in the average conversation, the language of celebration tends to sound less like street talk and more like some sort of ritual. However, the rituallike language of true celebration is far from otherworldly or unreal. It gives adequate expression, in fact, to the grand human emotions which crave a voice, all too often in vain. It is because of this need that Blacks and many others have never surrendered the majestic phrases of the King James Version, and that the oratory in the writing of an Apostle Paul can speak for them despite his culture-bound silence on the sin of slavery. The tongue of soul celebration must needs be beautiful and special.

Beauty is important not only in verbal celebration but in the sounds, the movements, and the figures used. Pitch, tonality, and artistic variety in vocal production are all aspects of beauty contributing to celebration. The intoned Black sermon has very African cultural roots, but it survives and is beloved because it provides, *today,* a means of expression which is more varied and powerful and beautiful. Intonation gives the gospel more "wave lengths." It is viewed as ugly only because of deep-seated cultural bias. However, even when the ordinary seems ugly, true celebration may lift up its beauty of function and make it the prevalent impact. For instance, there is an unmistakable beauty about Isaiah's portrayal of the Messiah as resembling a root out of dry ground (Isa. 53:2). The pursuit of his point about the superficial unloveliness of the Saviour gives celebration-level dignity to the most unlovely countenance in the congregation. It can generate joy from every position on the totem pole of pulchritude, bottom to top. The celebration-worship of the Lord must needs be "in the *beauty* of holiness" (Psalm 96:9).

Needless to say, the symbolic use of the ordinary and the need for poetic statement and other forms of beauty all lead unerringly to the imaginative. One does not celebrate in rigidly literal terms. The soul is free to soar and to create its offering of praise from the inevitable raw materials of earth, but they are lifted to the dimensions of dreams and visions. To celebrate one's God-given existence on earth is not to be chained to it, but to see beyond it, and indeed to dwell on a plane of transconscious transcendence. God's presence in the life of the person firmly rooted in this world is hopelessly impossible to describe in any literal vehicle of expression. But the poetic and the imaginative can give utterance to the unspeakable. And is not this unspeakable the greatest cause of all for celebration?

A final suggestion about celebrative material is that is must deeply involve the speaker. As we have seen earlier, whether it be a personal experience, a scene from the Bible, or a story from somewhere else, the preacher must be *in* the characters; and this involvement must beget celebration in the pulpit *first*. I suspect it is no idle happenstance that priests have been referred to historically as the "celebrants." The preacher who would lead in celebration must lead in celebrat*ing*— in freely expressing the feelings which characterize the act. No preaching material in and of itself is likely to be so powerful as to overcome a flat and feelingless delivery in detachment. Celebration is *contagious;* it is caught after it is taught. But how shall the epidemic be launched if the preacher is culturally inoculated with inhibitions against demonstrative, joyous praise and celebration?

Here, then, are some examples of material which lends itself well to the uses of celebration, particularly in sermon conclusions. It falls mainly into three categories: (1) Scripture, both in direct quotation and in creative paraphrase; (2) hymns and poetry; and (3) very moving personal experiences, both of oneself and of others. Some sermonic climaxes, of course, may combine two or even all three of these types of material. These illustrations of types were skimmed from my own sermon file.

The whole of the Bible, particularly the King James Version, is rich in rhetorical eloquence and poetic statement. The Psalms are full of declarations which can be delivered verbatim in celebrational dimensions. One of my most memorable conclusions came from Psalm 103. I introduced it with unavoidably deep feelings as I told of standing beside the hospital bed of an ancient saint who was supposed to be passing on. His daughter suggested that I quote his favorite Psalm. I pulled out my ever-ready, little (but complete) Bible and started to read. But he was way ahead of me as his mute but expressive lips formed the words in anticipation:

> Bless the Lord, O my soul: and all that is within me, bless his holy name. Bless the Lord, O my soul, and forget not all his benefits: who

forgiveth all thine iniquities; who healeth all thy diseases; who redeemeth thy life from destruction; who crowneth thee with loving kindness and tender mercies; . . . Bless the Lord, all his works in all places of his dominion; bless the Lord, O my soul.

He was my wife's father.

The prophets provide moving statements also. James Sanders's statement on the theme of the great invitation was distributed nationally on cassette. It inspired for me a sermon on excuses. The prophetic criticism dealt with bad priorities, but the positive conclusion dealt with the festive or celebrative nature of the truly Christian life. The very natural summation was a nearly verbatim quotation of Isaiah 55:1–3, followed by Black-culture restatements in like style. From the tape it sounded like this:

> Wherefore do ye spend money for that which is not bread? And your labour for that which satisfieth not? Hearken diligently unto me, and eat that which is good, and let your soul delight itself in fatness. Ho, *every* one that thirsteth, come ye to the waters, and he that hath no money; come ye, buy, and eat; yea come, buy wine and milk without money and without price. Incline your ear, and come unto me: hear, and your soul shall live; and I will make an everlasting covenant with you, even the sure mercies of David.
>
> How come you spend your money for stuff you can't even eat, and how come you scuffle and hustle for things that never *will* satisfy that something within? Listen to me, and fill up on a menu that is *really* good; and let your soul eat until you want no more. Lookahere, *every*body that's honest enough to know you're hungry and thirsty, come to the fountain; and you that know you ain't got *nothin'* where you really need it most, come on, buy and eat. Come and buy wine and milk without money and without even a price tag. God says, "Bend you ear and come to me. *Listen,* and your soul shall live, even in these dry and starving times."

Of course there is no more appropriate a climax and vehicle of celebration than the creative and imaginative narration of a whole biblical story. I did a sermon once on being really sorry for the evils we do against people and society and against God.

The conclusion was an expanded retelling of the text, in full color. The result was an experience of celebration. In this rendition of Luke 22:54–62, the audience was helped to see that these tears were a breakthrough to repentance and to victory:

> Peter had problems that morning early, as he stood in the palace courtyard. While Jesus was getting his lynch-trial justice inside, Peter was lonesome, and he looked around for his usual audience to lead. He had been accustomed to being recognized, and he had extreme ego needs. He had been the *boss* among the fisherman, and he was the leader of the disciples, next to Jesus. He *enjoyed* things like speaking to thousands and telling them to be seated.
>
> The only folks around that morning were the ones standing by the fire. So he joined this bunch and started talking and making his moves. Right away a girl spotted him for a Jesusite. Here he was, trying to sort of take over some new turf, and this janitor/maid has to spoil it all talkin' 'bout "This man was with Jesus." Peter spoke before he thought, and he said, "I don't even know the man."
>
> Well, it worked for a little while, but somebody else accused him a little later of being from the Jesus bunch. Peter was so set on joining this new bunch that he "woofed" at the fellow: "Man, I am not!" So then he stood there and tried to work his way in for a whole hour, and he thought he was getting away big. But the people kept listening to his Galilean accent, and they knew *some*thing was wrong. Finally somebody said, "Come on now, you were with him, for you are a Galilean, and your very talk gives it away and betrays you." Peter was really upset, and he cussed and swore (cf. Mt. 26:72) and said, "I don't know what you're talking about!" It was like saying, "Man, I ain't never been down Souf' "
>
> And just that second he heard the rooster crowing, and he looked up just in time to see Jesus looking him dead in the eye. He remembered what Jesus had said, and he couldn't hardly *stand* it!
>
> There was Jesus' knit brow silently saying, "I'm having an *awful* time, and even *you*'ve denied me." And there was his set jaw saying, "But I'm prepared for the worst, and I'll not give in." And worst of all there were Jesus' loving and penetrating eyes. They spoke worlds of deep meaning. They said, "I know, Peter; I understand. Didn't I say it would be like this? But don't worry, Peter, I still love you anyway. *Thanks,* Peter, for even coming this far with me. Now goodbye, Peter." It was too much! Peter couldn't take it any more.

And Peter went out and cried like a baby. The big, strapping, cussing, talkative fisherman walked away and *cried!*

But he never denied Jesus again. He went back to his fishing, but in his next real test he said, "Let me tell *you* something. You can beat me if you want to, or even kill me. But the man was healed by Jesus. He's the one you big shots crucified; and he's like the stone that the builders rejected and it became the keystone of the arch. Now go ahead and do what you want to do. I'll *never* deny him again (Acts 4:5-12).

The rest of this work is devoted to a kind of unpacking of the three preceding chapters, spelling out in detail the implications of personal experience and celebration as generated in folk culture. The major illustration of this approach is, of course, taken from the Black preaching tradition. Components such as the Bible as oral tradition, the folk dialogue of preaching, and even the folk language are treated, before the meaning of the entire work is summed up in a consideration of the recovery of a strong preaching tradition.

5. Preaching as Biblical Storytelling

THE HUGE place of the Bible in the recovery of preaching must be described in terms dealing with total life-style, culture and world view. Indeed, preaching will have to play a great part in the recovery of the place of the Bible in contemporary culture, in order to achieve in turn its own optimum function as a means of proclaiming the gospel. In other words preaching has fallen on evil days, not alone because of its own content and method, but also because it cannot be done in a theological or biblical vacuum. The underlying assumption of the approach proposed here is drawn, of course, from Black religious culture and experience, but the place given the Bible may well be the dream of every devout Christian of every culture and of most schools of Christian thought as well. Without such a central place assumed and sought for the Bible, it may well be asked why anybody would bother to attempt the recovery of preaching.

Despite all the varieties of Christian tradition for dealing with the Bible, there is no competing belief-base given serious consideration anywhere, whether creedal, theological or institutional. The staying power of the Bible throughout Christendom is itself testimony to the power of its message. The scope of its readership is as wide as the occurrence of the name Christian, and even the very simple preeminence of the Bible which I propose here is not wanting for wide support. My very first attempt to teach a Black approach to biblical material was made at a Roman Catholic diocesan seminary, and the interest of the future priests has not been surpassed in the intervening years. Religious Science no less than Pentecostal, all have reacted enthusiastically to the possibilities proposed through the recovery of a vital biblical message.

THE PRIMACY OF THE ORAL

The centrality of the biblical tradition suggested here is a challenge to reclaim the dynamics of Old Testament and primitive Christian processes for the sharing of the heritage. It is a call to the recovery of a living, transgenerational, oral religious tradition, rather than a stereotypical promotion of bibliolatry—bondage to print literalism. The oral processes, long lost in most Western societies because of the advent of the printing press, have survived amazingly well in such places as West Africa. And the Black Church in America has been built not on the literacy denied slaves and their descendants, but on the African cultural bias for massive memory, lively renditions/"readings" and supportive situational sharing, whether in ceremony or simple conversation. The early biblical method of verbally passing on the history/gospel is alive and well today, mostly unidentified as such among the very people who practice it best.

It should come as no surprise, of course, that the process of oral tradition proposed here is actually the early church's method. The real surprise should be in the huge significance attached unconsciously and on a culture-wide basis to print as an almost all-out replacement for human-to-human heritage transmission. Even sophisticated hermeneutical systems tend to deal with isolated print with such dead seriousness as to lose the highly personal impact of an oral "document" in the folk category, as opposed to a scholarly treatise for meticulous analysis. The purposes of the original folk-level corpuses of material included the religious nurture of the young, the rectification and stabilization of society, and once Christianity had emerged as a counterculture the commitment of individuals to follow Christ in saving faith and loyal obedience. History and good news were valued not as an end in themselves but for these more pragmatic purposes. Without losing the serious priesthood of all believers and several other values which have evolved from the printing press, we must now regain the chief locus for the lively storage of the tradition: the minds and hearts of the believers, individually and as whole churches and social groupings. The Bible must be given living storage alongside the objective and abstract images which are maintained in suspended animation on paper and all too often in sermons, lectures and other common religious communications.

This is another way of saying that bestseller status is good, but the Holy Book's contents must be made the topics of godly gossip—the stuff of the animated conversations of parents and children, husbands and wives, and larger family groupings in the spirit. The Deuteronomic priests were aware that the best way to keep their faith and values alive was to install it casually and interestingly in the every day chatter of Hebrew households. "And these words, which I command thee this day, shall be in thine heart: and thou shalt teach them diligently unto thy children, and shalt talk of them when thou sittest in thine house, and when thou walkest by the way, and when thou liest down, and when thou risest up" (Deut. 6:7). All this in *addition* to printing it and carrying it about! But those priests would have had no tradition with which to work in the first place had this oral practice not already prevailed for many generations. Biblical preaching must be recovered not as a scintillating occupation for professional preachers, but as a resource feeding the folk processes of the people of God. Alongside the bright ideas so dear to Western homileticians there must be recovered a meaningful set of biblical, spiritual folk heroes and happenings which set forth in vivid symbol the truths so impossible to capture adequately in direct rational address.

AUTHORITY IN ORAL TRADITION

Increased emphasis on oral tradition is not only well precedented in the history but functionally desirable in our own time. Those who fear that the authority and accuracy of Scripture might be undermined in so unstructured a folk process have but to look at the cultures whose values and world view are still communicated exclusively by oral tradition. One could easily generalize that values passed down orally are better maintained and more normative by far in the behavior of their respective societies. Whatever the reasons for the erosion of the authority of tradition in industrial, print-oriented societies, certainly no one would dare suggest that oral tradition is anything less than the best basis for preserving the authority of a tradition. Spoken heritage is part and parcel of the authority of the nuclear and extended family over their young—involved in the instruction for their very survival, having developed from the experience of the centuries.

Once we are agreed on the need to establish the authority of scriptural values and world view among folk generally, we have limited choices as to how it shall be achieved. On the one hand there is a tradition in which parent, preacher, or teacher heralds the authority, rigid or flexible, of a printed document. This holy writ serves as historical and theological basis for Christian faith and work, but the very abstractness of it separates it from the largely nonrational dynamics of daily life. Whole persons can hardly be constrained transconsciously and saved by such. On the other hand there is a tradition in which concrete validation in the persons of parents, pastors, and significant others has always generated overwhelming authority. The sacred story has never been separable from those who enjoyed not only talking and sharing it, but walking and practicing it as well. They, as ancestors ancient and contemporary, have given the tradition whatever authority they had. Thus it is impossible to speak of the God of Abraham and Isaac and Jacob without also speaking of their life style and world view.

This style of transgenerational and transconscious tradition is especially well exemplified in the religious tradition of the masses of Blackamerica, and it is testified to in the writings of important Blackamericans. Despite his early penchant for Western learning, Dr. Benjamin E. Mays prayed and prayed by night and day for the opportunity to obtain an education. He did this because of the authority which his mother's oral traditional upbringing exercised over a young man, even though he rebelled against much of the injustice traditionally accepted.[1] Dr. Howard Thurman's classic volume on *Jesus and the Disinherited* shows the influence of an oral traditional authority established in connection with the Bible, as inherited from his ex-slave grandmother, who cared for him during much of his childhood. To all intents and purposes, the *real* Bible for the grandson was that portion which his grandma loved and quoted and had him to read to her.[2] Its authority went far beyond respect for print, for it was summed up in the awe and love commanded by a towering spiritual giant called grandma. Even a versatile artist like Maya Angelou, hardly to be identified with the institutional church, illustrates the power of the oral religious tradition in Black culture. Her compelling autobiographical novel, *I Know Why the Caged Bird Sings,* is loaded with evidence of her familiarity with the Bible, and its influence on her world view.[3] Quite obviously its place in her life was more the result of informal oral communication within the family than of the impact of preachers held in light esteem, or of church school teachers hardly mentioned. With Angelou, as with Mays and Thurman, the richness and commanding influence of the Bible were wrapped in living epistles who interpreted life, on the spot, in biblical terms. It was this identical process which kept African Traditional Religion intact and authoritative through lengthened centuries, and which preserved biblical sources and their influence on Hebrew life until committed to writing.

The tragedy for modern society is the fact that we have lost, for the most part, the folk-oral parallels to the sources of Hebrew and Greek documents. The authority possible in print is only a very limited substitute for the transconscious impact of a word/ event between persons. The most likely instrument for recovering the process and returning scripture to a major place in daily conversation and decision is preaching. The most promising single means of acculturation toward the recovery of the Bible as a lively and authoritative folk document is its folk rendition, with power, in preaching.

Twenty-five years ago a young Black preacher was given the task of leading worship in a camp for delinquents and predelinquents, at 7:30 in the morning. Few audiences could have had more need for an authoritative word in their lives, and few would have had less preparation on which to build that word. Compulsory attendance only made matters worse, yet the log seats by the brook filled early after the first morning. Black, White, and Brown alike, male and female, with few exceptions, looked forward to the tale to be told, and they could be heard discussing it the rest of the day. The secret of this popularity lay in the lively folk character of the Bible stories that were told, and in the clear applications of these stories to their lives. This relevance and interest reached its peak one morning early in the second week, after a twelve-year-old girl had nearly opted to leave camp out of horrible embarrassment. She had both personal experience and court records enough for a thirty-five year old, but she was deeply hurt when she found that a group of boys from her town had gathered to compare intimate responses to her charms. The violent threats of one loyal boy had put the gossip to a stop, and some counselors had helped with such as "How would you like for somebody to talk about *your* sister that way?" But the issue had not died, and it hung like a dark cloud over Angela especially. Then rose the preacher casually to tell his tale in the clipped, gutteral accent of his former home in Brooklyn. It went something like this:

> Once there was this pretty girl. She was really fine, but she was raggedy and poor, and there wasn't no good jobs in factories or offices or telephone companies or nothing like that. If you didn't have no store or street stall to sell things of your own, you was just

out of luck. So this pretty girl got a job scrubbing in the palace. It was awful hard work and she wasn't very strong, but she and her little brothers and sisters needed that money bad.

One morning she was about to knock off the job when this dude walked up to her and said, "Baby, what you doing slaving like this? They ain't paying you nothing, and besides your pretty arms and legs wasn't made for no such hustle as this. Just look at your hands! Why don't you come with me? You can take it easy and make yourself some long green too."

Well, to make a long story short, she went with this dude and soon she was in the streets selling herself. At first it didn't seem too bad and the money sure was handy. It wasn't all that much, but it was so much better than those palace maid wages, and her kid brothers and sisters were eating regular now. But she felt worse and worse about her hustle, and there was times when she felt lower than a snake's belly. She felt dirty, and she felt like all those men were dirtier than she was. She got where she almost hated to see a man or to walk on the street, 'cause they never looked at anything but her body—right through clothes and all.

Then one day she met this prophet-type named Jesus, and he was real different. He looked at her too, but his look didn't stop where other guys did. When he smiled at her he wasn't hittin' on her for nothing; he just liked her, like you like your best friend. She felt so good she didn't know what to do. Whenever she could, she followed Jesus and listened to what he was teaching. One day she followed him to the house of a church bigshot, where he was invited to dinner. In those days houses were more open, and people was always crashing parties. It wasn't no big thing when this pretty girl followed Jesus in. He stretched out on a sofalike chair, with his feet away from the table, and then this pretty girl did some strange things. She was crying hard and she took her tears and washed the dust off of Jesus' feet. Then she dried them with her pretty long hair and, get this, she *kissed* his feet. Then she topped it all off by rubbing them with perfumed oil—the same expensive stuff she used for herself. In fact this was probably her last perfume, and she was putting it on Jesus' feet because she wouldn't need it no more. She had decided to change her whole life, and that's why she had been crying so much.

Well, the host, this bigshot from the church, was taking it all in. He was thinking, "I thought this guy was supposed to be a great prophet; he doesn't even know this woman is a prostitute. Because if he did, he sure wouldn't let her get all that familiar." Jesus saw the look in his eye and knew just what he was thinking. So he said, "I got something to tell you," and the host said, "Go right ahead." Then Jesus laid this story on him. "Once there was this money lender that had two guys that owed him money. One of them owed him five hundred dollars, and the other one owed him fifty. Didn't either one of them pay, 'cause they didn't have any money, so he got kind-hearted and just told them to skip it. Tell me, Simon (that was the name of the host), which one of these dudes do you think would like the money lender the most?" Simon answered and said, "I suppose that the guy that he forgave the most money." And Jesus said to him, "You said right," then he turned to the woman and said to Simon, "You see this woman? I came to your house, you didn't wash my feet with no water, dusty though they were, but she washed my feet with tears and wiped them with the hairs of her head. You didn't give me no kiss, no warm greeting, but this woman ever since I have been here hasn't stopped caressing my feet. A lot of people put oil on your head when you come to their house, but you didn't do it, and yet this woman put perfumed oil on my *feet*. So I want you and her both to know that whatever she has done that was wrong I sure forgive her, for she has loved much. But those that don't think they got a whole lot to be forgiven, they don't love me very much." And then Jesus said to the woman "Your sins are forgiven."[4]

This story was followed with a brief account of a church and shrine built in the Caribbean Islands by a group of women like this same woman. Needless to say, the attention had been more rapt than ever, but the most important change in the audience was the tears that met under the chin of Angela. This message in folk story had given her the authority of God for forgiveness of her own sins, and her burden was lifted and she finished up the camp period with a heart perhaps lighter than she had had for many months or years.

The presentation concluded with a very brief hint that a great deal of the story told could be found in the last part of the seventh chapter of Luke's Gospel; and counselors were known to be asked to verify that such a story was actually in the Bible. The relevance and compelling authority of the gospel were welcomed, and, in their own shy way, these biblical illiterates sensed the importance of the fact that the tale told in Brooklynese was in fact taken from that Holy Book called the Bible.

LIVELY PREACHING AND ORAL TRADITION

Whatever scholarly and other criticisms may be brought to bear against the tale recorded above, it could hardly be called dull. The language as printed was supplemented by gesture, facial expression and vocal intonation, and emphasis for a lively rendition. The attention given was rapt. So has it always been with the important stories of a serious tradition. From Samson and David to Beowulf and beyond, the folk tales that have *lived* have been lively and interesting, as well as instructive of the values of the society out of which they came. The Euro-American assumption that profundity must be dull has never disturbed these "primitive" societies. The genius of oral tradition is that it *assumes* an interesting performance which relates immediately to life and its needs. It cannot depend on a piece of paper to hold its content; it has to hold its audience.

At the level of worship in Black religion, both of the elements most appealing to the audience are oral: music and preaching. Theological orthodoxy and literary elegance have nowhere near the same effect on attendance as authentic soul sermons and songs. Yet orthodoxy·may not be violated in the interest of liveliness. Much like the earlier African model, most Black-american audiences are much too familiar with the oral tradition of the Bible to permit glaring error. Liveliness in authentic folk tradition is *an addition* and not an alternative to faithfulness to the tradition. Appeal is based on both accuracy and lively rendition.

Many of the best-known jokes in Black folklore poke fun at ignorance of the traditions. In Africa as well as Black America, it is assumed that ignorance of the folk heritage is all but inexcusable. In America this folklore is Christian as well as what might be called common. R. M. Dorson, Professor of Folklore at Indiana University, records a hilarious tale where two backsliding deacons have been away from church so long that one of them couldn't recall the titles Lord and Christ for Jesus.[5] The effect of the tale reported was greatly enhanced by the lively rendition of how the backslider received his cues while in the midst of prayer. But the implication that people ought to know their tradition was quite clear, as in the vast majority of folktales in Black culture.

Dorson was fascinated by the "insights into Negro storytelling" gained at a "Negro Baptist Revival" in Arkansas.[6] What he encountered was the simple fact that folk tradition has no arbitrary boundaries between sacred and secular—that the same style of storytelling prevailed at churches, barbershops, and street corners. In fact the pulpit was perhaps more a source than a product of both style and content in the field of much of the folk material.

The traditional Black pulpit thus radiates influence because of its folk interpretation of the Bible, which was itself originally a folk document, and because that folk interpretation is, like all authentic folk materials, relevant and lively. Dorson seeks to define the elements of that liveliness. He mentions the "intoned prayer, the rhythmic cry, the chanted phrase and the religious lyric," the antiphonal response, mimicry, and the "uncanny reproduction of sounds"—"sound effects that a radio technician would envy." Note is taken of the fact that Black storytellers "gesticulate and act out parts in exciting narrations" with performances dramatic in nature.[7] What Dorson failed to report was the fact that folk preachers are no less lively in their most serious moments, so the dramatic impact of the Bible is not restricted to the humorous. The richness of the folk interpretation is functional throughout the spectrum of religious concern.

Purely religious concerns, of course, are about real life—the actual experiences of persons. The high impact of oral tradition is accomplished, so to speak, by reruns of segments of real life. Dorson reflects this fact when he expresses a kind of surprise that "many Negro narratives are told as true personal experiences.[8] I have long referred to this phenomenon as the "eyewitness account." Anything short of such a complete rerun can hardly generate an experience that teaches and moves persons. "Eyewitnesses" describe settings that are vivid and familiar. Congregations quickly visualize and relate to the situation, moving into the experience. The best of biblical scholarship should be used in the development of folksy detail, but it comes alive because it already lives in the teller. I was impressed recently by the truth of this assertion during a revival in a poorer section of the Black ghetto to the south of Los Angeles. Utilizing the bicentennial theme and focusing on equality before God, the sermon was designed to build healthy pride and strong self image. To my amazement, a casually detailed portrayal of a familiar scene almost caused people to rise up out of their seats. The simple description of a setting can be extremely effective:

> Jesus told a story about laborers hired to work in a vineyard. I can see the picture. When I was a pastor in the cotton country there was a certain block where there were people standing around all the time—*any* hour. And most of them were not leisure class. Leisurely folk don't dress like they did. Some had paper sack lunches, but they were looking for no picnic. But you could tell what they were about if you would go down to the block at four or five o'clock in the morning, just before day, a big old raggedy bus would pull through there, and a man would hire folks to chop cotton. If you would watch long enough sometimes, the bus would come again and fill up again. They would work a long day in the fields and the bus would bring them back to the block around six or seven o'clock at night. Well this is the way it was. Jesus said the man hired a load and took them to the field. But he saw it wasn't enough, so he came back in the block three hours later and hired some more. It still wasn't enough and he hired still some more. And again, even in midafternoon, and finally just an hour before quitting time, he came and hired some more.[9]

As I moved on to the conclusion of the story there was a fleeting moment when I wondered why all the excitement. But it dawned on me later that a sizable number of my congregation were even more familiar than I was with the cotton fields and with the blocks where casual labor was hired. They also knew the Bible tradition rather well. They were so responsive because they had easily moved into the well-known setting and were already anticipating and celebrating a fresh and much-needed awareness of God-given dignity and equality, even among seasonal laborers and the unemployed.

"Eyewitnesses" likewise establish folk characterizations that are intimate and life scale. The nonrational sector of the transconscious says immediately, "I know that fellow!" The subject may be a character from the early Old Testament, but the visceral response is, "I been knowin' that lady ever since I was a little kid." Dr. Sandy F. Ray must have thousands of these people with whom to make sermon events into real-life experiences. At the 1976 Baptist Congress of Christian Education in San Francisco I saw one of his characters better than big screen and full color:

> We recognize that the disciples were pushing for power. They had had people lording over them all their lives—they had been bossed all of their days. And now they wanted to be bosses themselves. Jesus sensed that several times. On one occasion people were disputing over who was going to be boss—who was going to be the head person when he came into his empire. They thought they could see that he was moving toward becoming king, and they were getting ready. They wanted to be assigned as officials in the empire. Who was going to be head?
>
> There was a very dedicated woman, you remember, who went to him because she had two sons—like Brother Williams here has two fine sons. And she went to Jesus and said, "Look, Jesus, when you come into your kingdom—when you get into your power—I want to talk to you now because I know it is going to be rushed and mean after you get in. There'll be lots of folks pushing and shoving. But I want to get to you now, because you know my sons—you know me and you know my sons. You know I've dedicated them. You know me, and I want to get to you now before the crowd gets around you. When you get into the kingdom, Sir, let one of my sons sit on the right hand and the other on the left."
>
> They were power hungry, and this was the only power they knew anything about.

The teller gave the impression that he was moving effortlessly among numberless remembered details from which he selected the proper ones, avoiding cluttering up the character unnecessarily. Without seeing the mother's face or hair or height, one saw her typical motherly concern to see that her children got ahead in the world. We *all* knew that woman because Dr. Ray knew her so well, and we were ready for the punch line when it came.

"Eyewitnesses" also describe action in ways that are close to folk experiences and concerns. Dr. Ray's sermon to a Kansas City congregation on the occasion of their eightieth anniversary consisted of a candid appraisal of churches. For his license to be so candid in evaluation, he described Jesus' cleansing of the temple from his typical, folksy, inside and insightful perspective:

> The temple was originally designed for spiritual purposes. And Jesus was annoyed by what he found when he went into the temple. He saw creeping materialism that had watered down the spiritual power of the church. When he saw the selling of doves, pigeons, and heifers, and the changing of money on the outside, Jesus dared to cleanse it as his house. Think of this! Here's a young preacher from Nazareth who only had a few country people and village people, and they didn't have any of the power and the money, and *he* had no money. But he stands up in the temple—and I doubt seriously if he had paid any money for the construction of this temple, because he didn't have it. And he stands in this temple and says my house—*my* house. I bet he hadn't paid for a stone, he just didn't have any money, and there was no money much in Nazareth either. They were pilgrims that came down from Nazareth, and the trip cost a lot, so they couldn't bring with them a lot of money. This temple was undoubtedly built by the monied people of the great city of Jerusalem. But Jesus comes down out of Nazareth, just a country preacher, and stands in the temple in the midst of all these scribes and Pharisees and says *"My* house!" "My house because you claim my father's name. My house because you built it in the name of my Father. It's my house because my Father and I are one, and it's my house—not the material—but the purpose and design and the name in which you built it. This makes it my house."

There followed a use of the building figure in which Jesus declared that the spiritual building had serious violations. Minds were open to this searching spiritual inspection because poor people identified with the audacity and the validity of Jesus who was poor like themselves. When the same Jesus would soon be inspecting their own eighty-year-old spiritual house, this action so colorfully portrayed would be far more acceptable and meaningful. Prophetic judgment was experienced in familiar concretes, and the action was real in the life of the hearers, having been real in the mind and life of the folk-storyteller preacher.

The question that must be answered now is, "How much does this say to most of the White church or even to the Black middle-class church?" It is obvious that few White audiences would suddenly accept such an informal folk approach from the mouths of their own ministers, even if they were enchanted by it from the mouth of some Black from outside their circle. In their minds, the style is tinged with primitivity and tainted with undertones of ignorance. Under such circumstances a hearer is entertained, but not taught—not given a living, growing experience. Yet once the false cultural inhibitions are removed, there can be no better proclamation of the gospel than that which lives in vivid heroes, heroines, and life situations.

This seems like turning back the clock of culture and negating intellectual progress. But the fact is that it is only facing reality. We have never stopped having flesh-and-blood-type heroic symbols. The hue and cry against violence on television is raised only because it peoples the minds of children with the wrong heroes, heroines, and violent activities. These still have great influence on the young, and indeed on the whole population. What Black tradition offers is simply a model for equal time or better—a way of giving back to the culture the Bible figures lost to most White Americans, especially outside the South.

I saw the last vestiges of America's Bible heritage in the North in my home city of Columbus, Ohio, in the early 1930s. The Junior High Torch Clubs of the City YMCA held annual Bible storytelling contests, but the glory of the early contests had fled. The contests were duller and duller, and the popularity of David and Samson, to the exclusion of the other Bible characters, rendered the program all the more monotonous. My excellent (20/20) hindsight now tells me that the decline of the contests came because they were no longer the natural products of the culture. Boys at puberty were constructing their own Bible stories without any culturewide or even pulpitwide help from adults. Radio-nurtured boys chose heroes from the Bible on the basis of their usefulness in portraying the Western values of violence and competition, into which they had already been repaganized by nonbiblical heroes on the radio. David and Samson were only vehicles for the expression of a culturewide world view which was already spiritually dead. So the contest became a mockery, far removed from the stature of Scripture. Acculturation back to the Bible-based world view will take great scholarship and prodigious imagination, as well as many years. But there is no better place to start than in the professional pulpit, and no better time to start than now. Story art has never lost its universal appeal; it needs only to be informed by truth and used with skill as never before.

ORAL TRADITION AS THEOLOGICAL SOLUTION

A final word is in order about the recovery of oral biblical traditions in preaching, as a promising solution to the theological wars which have rent the body of Christ for centuries. In addition to its superior access to the less accessible sectors of the transconscious, and its livelier and better claim on the attention of audiences, the revival of an oral-traditional approach offers a return to "primitive," preprint orthodoxy, which transcends or dissolves the issues between liberal and conservative—modernist and fundamentalist—and lets the Bible live again.

Alongside the word in chapter 2 about the perils of warring against the revivalist factors which helped form the culture and psyche of mainstream White America, there is a positive word to be said about expanding the ranks of those who love and quote the Scripture on a dynamic folk basis. The intellectual criteria of the late twentieth century will not permit a literal duplication of ancient oral uses of Scripture, but the basic approach can be very similar. And the inevitable changes can be to the good, strengthening and enlightening the impact of the Bible today, as compared with earlier times.

The subtle errors and arrogance of Western culture have cost the religious world much. Perhaps the chief example is literalism, not exclusively as found among an obscurantist religious minority today, but also among the whole Euro-American intellectual establishment. The error lies in the assumption that things can literally be reduced to words and captured there in completeness. It is the error of acting as if a problem has been solved when it has only been given a name with a Latin stem. It is the arrogance of putting approximations and abstractions into logical syllogisms and holding the results of such human manipulations to be absolute. The understanding of African and Black American culture has suffered much at the hands of such, and the very well-being of Blacks has been assaulted by theological rationalizations of slavery and contemporary self-centered, culturebound interpretations which support a world of rampant inequities. But the depths of human insight and religious awareness inside the Euro-American family itself have suffered no less. The resulting theological wars have sapped the strength of the Christian church and divided its forces and witnesses in a tragic manner. Arguments tend to relate to man-made abstractions and absolutist stances on interpretation. Few if any of the controversies over Scripture itself or any of the doctrines would have lasted very long if focused on the kinds of issues people face in real life. In other words, the life meanings of the Bible, for which it was handed down orally in the first place, have seldom been at issue. And the return to those existential applications of scripture would defuse the divisions.

Of course these charges of arrogant absoluteness are not new, and to the extent that they are already perceived correct, efforts have been and are being made to correct them. But the discouraging fact is that new schools of understanding the Bible itself are so caught up in analytical technicalities that the deadening literalism which haunts liberal and conservative alike continues to reign in fresh disguise. One school of thought denies or destroys much of the Bible by reason of the literalistic misunderstandings of what it is and what it means; the other extreme destroys the Bible by forcing reality to bend to an idol of paper and ink.

The point is simply that the authors and The Author had no such usage in mind. Persons immersed in history and in touch with God told their children what they learned about living under God, and they used a story method. They had no illusions about being able to describe their experiences in meticulous scientific detail, but they found their method adequate to guide person's lives and indeed the decisions of whole groups. These early recorder/interpreters did not always agree with each other in every particular, but they had no arrogant compulsion to destroy each other's work in the interest of their own recognition. In fact, when they or their descendants got around to recording their stories in writing, they put various versions alongside each other in the canon without comment. They must have assumed that folk would get the needed messages on their own. In fact it was late in the development of the New Testament that John (14:26) recorded a statement in which Jesus acknowledged the express need for the Holy Ghost to be sent to help interpret what he had said. Jesus' own ministry was full of stories, almost none of which required interpretation afterwards. He apparently had the idea that the quaint, simple method of his culture was capable of conveying the greatest profundities, and the impact of his storytelling ministry speaks for itself.

Preaching which utilizes and perpetuates such a theologically noncontroversial, narrative-oriented style is to be found in many places in the earth. It is particularly alive and well in the Black church in America. Most of the best of Black preaching maintains depth and relevance by means of art rather than argument, and the product appeals to the White theological left as well as the right. The one typically wants to be sure that the ills of society are properly and seriously addressed, while the other demands that the Bible be taken very seriously. The broadness of this folk appeal obviously owes something to its Black culture roots, but the major credit must go to the *biblical* oral tradition, with which African oral tradition was easily blended and extended. The *theological* solution prevails, regardless of how one assesses the cultural roots of an approach which depends on the symbolic significance of concrete accounts, rather than the uncertain accuracy and appeal of abstractions.

As Jesus suggested, *some* interpretation is needed, and this may border on the theological. But he recommended the Holy Ghost as capable of providing understanding for each in his own culture and capacity. Human assistance may be best utilized in the scholarly and imaginative reproduction of the theologically significant story. Editorial biases and tilts are possible in this process also, but the greatest danger lies in the direct interpretation. Theology has been the servant of the status quo far more than of the Holy Spirit, and that all too often unbeknown to the theologians themselves. The magnificent abolitionist orator/preacher, Sojourner Truth, was illiterate. Her approach to Scripture is instructive:

> I had forgotten to mention, in its proper place, a very important fact, that as she (Sojourner Truth) was examining the Scriptures, she wished to hear them without comment; but if she employed adult persons to read them to her, and she asked them to read a passage over again, they invariably commenced to explain, by giving her their version of it; and in this way they tried her feelings exceedingly. In consequence of this, she ceased to ask adult persons to read the Bible to her, and substituted children in their stead. Children as soon as they could read distinctly, would re-read the same sentence to her, as often as she wished, and without comment; and in that way she was enabled to see what her own mind could make out of the record, and that, she said, was what she wanted, and not what others thought it to mean. She wished to compare the teachings of the Bible with the witness within her; and she came to the conclusion, that the spirit of truth spoke in those records.[9]

There is, of course, a strong theological position implied in the high place given the Scripture here by Sojourner Truth, but the source of the status assigned is not abstract theological reflection; it comes from the already mentioned African-American appropriation of an oral tradition in their new language, the English which they were forced to use. Frances W. Titus made effort to expose the electrical effect of Sojourner Truth on a huge White audience. The comments were not unlike those of the television commentator who tried to understand the electric effect of Congresswoman Barbara Jordan at the 1976 Democratic Party Convention, but she ventured into areas where no person in mass media would dare to have gone in this enlightened day. In the process, Ms. Titus's liberal stereotyping has preserved some shreds of truth forgotten even by many Blacks:

> It is the theory of some writers that to the African is reserved, in the later and palmier days of the earth, the full and harmonious development of the religious element in man. The African seems to seize on the tropical fervor and luxuriance of Scripture imagery as something native; he appears to feel himself to be of the same blood with those old burning, simple souls, the patriarchs, prophets and seers, whose impassioned words seem only grafted as foreign plants on the cooler stock of the occidental mind.[10]

The concern expressed in this work is to restore the Bible to its place as the cornerstone of oral and popular culture. It is not inhibited by the stereotypical view of the "occidental mind" stated above. Whatever literalistic limitations and other substantial shortcomings the prevailing culture may have are all amenable to change by adaptations and acculturation, spurred by a purposeful pulpit. As defenders of school children in Black ghetto schools have had to say unnumbered times, "There is no such thing as a culturally handicapped child. There are only culturally different children." So also is there no such thing as a culturally handicapped White student of the Christian faith. There are only culturally different people. Where Whites have been most influenced by African culture, people of the South have already fused the best of "primitive" Euro-American affinity for the Bible with the best of Black influence. Few Blacks will exceed the late Clarence Jordan, a White Southerner, in the movement to restore Scripture to a popular and influential place in the conversation and common life of America. I never teach a course in Black biblical interpretation without referring to Jordan, and his long playing records of the Parables. In addition to the fact that his work stands well in any Black pulpit, it is true that a Jordan Bible story is memorable in any culture.

Jesus told the story one time, of a very rich man who liked to give a big party and invite in a lot of his cronies and serve them mint juleps out under his big magnolia trees, and just be the real aristocrat old gentleman with his little goatee and his pince-nez glasses, and a very cultured fellow. And all the while he was putting on this party there was laid at his gate a poor man named Lazarus. Now the rich man never did like to see this poor fellow around, he always said, "My he's so awful looking, and he isn't even my color and he's dirty and filthy, and I wish I didn't have him hanging around me so much. And he got the idea that he would build a big high woven wire fence around his place so that when he had a party he could lock the gate and not let any of those unsightly beggars be around asking him for bread and draining his mint julep glasses.

So he built that kind of a fence and enjoyed his privacy for a number of years. But in due time the poor man, the beggar, died and was carried away to the other world. Also the rich man, as all rich men do, died and was carried away to the other world.

Now it so happened that in this other life things were completely reversed. The man who had been begging for bread found that he had plenty of bread. The poor beggar Lazarus, who was so lacking in friends, now found that he had plenty of friends. And Lazarus who had been so ostracized and segregated now found that he was in the fellowship of all of the people of God, among whom was the great old patriarch of the race, Abraham himself. And many a time Abraham would invite old Lazarus over to his house for an evening banquet of fried chicken, black-eyed peas, gravy, rice and collard greens.

Now it so happened that the rich man found that he no longer had his table set with all of the dainties and delicacies of the South. He found that he didn't even have a drink of water, and the temperature was unseasonably hot, and getting even worse, along with extremely high humidity. And in this rather parched state, the rich man said, "Ooh I wonder where my water boy is. *Boy!* Bring me some water!" And no boy comes. And finally he sees this old beggar that had peered through the woven wire fence back on earth with his hungry look, wanting a little bit of bread—he sees him over there at the table with all kinds of water and Pepsi Colas and cool drinks and everything, and he cries out to Mr. Abraham, "Please, would you send that boy over here with some water to rub over my tongue, because I am in deep agony in this high heat and high humidity."

Well, Mr. Abraham says to him, "You know, while you were alive you had all the good things, you had the good sections of town, you had the good streets, you had the good schools, you had the good political offices, you had the good income, and Lazarus had to take what was left; he just got the scraps when you got through. He got the sections of town that you didn't want, he got the streets that you no longer used. You shut him out, and he had to take what was left. Now it happens that things have been completely reversed; you are hungry and thirsty, and he is well fed and well watered. But the big problem is that there has been a big gulf dug between us and you, a *deep* ditch. Now I want to remind you that that ditch is as deep here as your fence was high on earth, and it's just as impenetrable. We can't cross this deep ditch which you dug to keep men like Lazarus out—you wanted to segregate him, you didn't want him around. You were successful, you shut him out, and now you want him to cross over—but there's no bridge, just a deep ditch and he can't get to you with the water to cool your tongue. Nor can you come to us, because you know when you dig a ditch it breaks up traffic both ways. He can't come to you and you can't come to us; you'll have to continue in your torment which is your doing."

Well one good thing about this old rich fellow, he did realize and was willing to confess his guilt. He said, "You know I have some brothers back there that are thinking just like I thought; they've got the same notions that I had. Would you please, since Lazarus can't come to me, would you please let him go back to earth to my brothers down there, and tell them how awful it is to break communications, how awful it is to dig gulfs between themselves and their fellowman, so that they won't come to this stage of torment that I'm in." And Abraham says, "Well, those people down there, they got the Baptist churches and the Methodist churches and Presbyterian churches and the Episcopalian churches, they got the preachers, they got the Bible. They got the freedom of assembly, the freedom of speech. Let them listen to the Bible and let them listen to the preachers, and let them do what the churches teach them to do." And this fellow says, "Oh no, they won't listen to the Bible, they won't listen to the preachers, but if you'll let Lazarus go back there and kinda scare the daylights out of them, maybe along late one Saturday night, I believe you'll get some action out of them, but they ain't going to listen to these preachers." And Abraham says, "Well, if they won't be persuaded to do right by the preachers and by the word of God, they won't be persuaded even though somebody goes to them from the dead."[11]

6. Preaching as Folk Language

THE LIVELY biblical rendition of Clarence Jordan is bound to raise the question of the appropriateness, for the worship of Almighty God, of folk language—nonstandard dialect, ungrammatical usage, and folk style. The more important question, however, is not what language matches one's Sunday clothes, but what patterns of speech penetrate the deepest and convey the most meaning transconsciously.

My own sensitivity to the issue is much greater than it once was because of experiences during and after my studies for a degree in Linguistics. The awareness came, however, outside the school setting and quite unexpectedly, as a result of candid comments by my congregation and other long familiar audiences. Because matters of this sort are often "below the level of conscious awarness"[1] (I would translate Labov to say "outside the sector of *rational* consciousness"), people explained themselves in precise religious terms such as: "Now you're really letting the Lord use you." Or, from outside my parish, "Since you left that office job and went into the pastorate, you're really preaching." The implication that I had been out of touch with God for the fourteen years I was an executive was not exactly what these kind souls had in mind, but it was there, along with their commendations for better understandability and impact.

Some went so far as to suggest that I had finally "gotten religion," or been converted. It was good to know that, in their minds, I had at last made contact, but fourteen years of previous failure were hard to take. Folks were saying that the kind words they gave me previously, throughout those fourteen years of sermons, were just kind words and no more. They inferred that I had been asked to preach those hundreds of times because of gratitude for the technical services I had rendered, in such things as building design and finance, or church incorporations and bylaws, or zoning petitions, or even finding a new pastor. It was humbling and shocking, especially since I was not conscious of changing anything at all. Certainly my theology, prayer life, and commitment to serious preparation for preaching had not changed one whit. What on earth then could make so many people mention this increased pulpit effectiveness?

The answer lay in the very subtleties of language which I was studying. The unconscious change in my speech was the direct result of days and days of research, in which I listened carefully to tapes of great Black preaching. The standard media English which I had learned in my midwestern birthplace had subtly evolved towards the mother tongue of the Black ghetto, especially when I was preaching. I had, without knowing it, *moved to avoid contrast with the preachers* whose sermons *I had admired* and analyzed for days, in connection with writing the thesis. I often maintained my old accent, as I noticed on my tapes, but I was now using one or more additional languages to preach— multilingually, if you please. The new tongue was never a deep watermelon accent or Amos-and-Andy dialect, but in a way very hard to define it was much more familiar to them. The social distance signaled by the exclusive use of the language of the oppressor was diminished, as elusive new shadings of pronunciation softened my hardness, once closely associated with boss talk. The typical but unintentional response to my appearance, even, was overcome. (As the Caucasoid product of coerced miscegenation during slavery, I am often mistaken for a non-Black on first sight. I had always stood in new pulpits amidst low and self-fulfilling expectations, since everybody in the ghetto fancies that White preachers "can't preach a lick.") The resistance I had never understood began to change when my language changed.

Needless to say, an improvement that dramatic deserved serious study. I still had some special problems, of course, but the lessons learned about language have developed into principles with broad applicability. In fact the very sermons I had studied were excellent models of the finding: the most learned and inspired ideas of the faith must be put not only into experience-centered narrative form, or folk-oral tales, but into the *folk language* of the people.

WHAT IS FORMAL/STANDARD, AND WHY?

If there is resistance to this assertion, it will likely stem from misunderstandings of what language is in the first place. The word language comes from the Latin word for tongue, and a language is a system of spoken communication, for which there may also be written symbols. Special systems of communication exist in national, regional, professional, and socioeconomic groups. In the 1970s, our most interesting new speech community is, as they are called, the C.B. (Citizen's Band) radio buff[2] community, whose colorful and compulsively inelegant private speech builds increasing millions into an intimate network of neighbors in the best American tradition. One volunteer subgroup alone has handled 55 million emergency calls in fourteen years. Try to tell a person whose life was saved that these people don't speak correctly! Of a true language it is only required that the people who speak it be able to understand each other.

Now of course the smaller the speech community, the narrower the usefulness of the language, but small is not automatically bad. The highly specialized language of ichthyologists is not to be scorned because their numbers are so few. However, therein lies the crux of the matter; ichthyological language is definitely not scorned, since despite its small number of speakers, it has professional *prestige*. The point is that languages are associated with groups, and people have unfortunately projected their feelings about groups onto their feelings about their languages, including the prestige of the very language they themselves speak:

> The development of linguistic insecurity has accompanied the development of the doctrine of correctness. In the seventeenth and eighteenth century, many rising members of the English middle class found themselves in social situations where their native speech patterns were not appropriate. It was this aspect of social mobility which created a need for a doctrine of correctness, and led to the elevation of the schoolmaster and the dictionary as authorities for speech in both England and America.[3]

The problems that stem from this emergence of social mobility are manifold. The linguistic insecurity which results from awareness of the language patterns of other groups can add to a host of other insecurities and undermine authentic personhood. But the chief evil, for our purposes, is the fact that language is misappropriated for an alien purpose: the signaling of real or imaginary social status.

So much significance is attached to this additional function of language that whole educations are centered on learning to speak and act like a "gentleman" or a "lady." Meanwhile, the original identity of the Pygmalion for whom Christ died is derided in a crushing manner, often by the person himself. There emerges from this morass not only the heresy of self-hatred but the equally damnable distance which language is used to signal between members of varying socioeconomic groups. One moves, without thinking it through, from an acceptable or standard speech pattern to an acceptable or standard identity. The question that rises to haunt us, then, is: What on earth is standard *identity?* And what language/identity should a preacher project to an ideally mixed or multiclassed congregation? Should one specialize in showing that one is educated, or should one emulate the incarnation, thinking it not robbery to signal closeness to persons of low estate?

TO SIT WHERE THEY SIT, AND SPEAK

One thing is certain; who one is perceived to be is now inextricably related to how one talks. Peter (Luke 22:55–62), seeking to join the servants by the fire, was excluded because his speech betrayed him to be a stranger (Matt. 26:73). From his first few phrases, his identity had been established, and the first impression was never overcome. He contrasted with the locals, and this involved many hazards. He was placed at a distance, associated with a leader to whom they were hostile, and not carefully listened to and understood, all because of his speech.

Preachers, on more serious business than Peter's business at the fire, still have these same hazards, and so does everybody else. Missed meanings are all too common because subtly different communication systems are being employed. Labov's research in the social stratification of language in New York City included tests of the acceptability of sounds.[4] Rather than to ask subjects directly, he had them evaluate hypothetical candidates for various levels of jobs, on the basis of their hearings of tapes of the candidates' reading. Imagine being rated $3000 to $5000 per year lower because of one's slightly deviant sound pattern! If that kind of importance attaches to language in job placement, how much more might a preacher's tongue influence the openness of souls to the saving gospel?

Since it is obvious that identity cannot be divorced from speech, the least one can do is to be sure that the personal image inevitably projected is as close as possible to the persons listening. With all the lowly save those who have polluted healthy, upward mobility with self-hatred, it is important that the preacher identify with the member of the lowest echelon in the congregation at a significant number of places in the sermon. It is also vital that preachers often identify linguistically with the *real* congregants, *all* of them, as opposed to the persons they seek to be, even though the preacher may also be a model of their upward goal. For many this may be threatening, especially if they have striven for all their lives to become such a model. I have found this particularly true of Black teachers attending seminars on linguistic and social distance. But the goal is not "bad" grammar or blood-curdling obscenities; it is the recovery or retention of nuances and subtleties of sound, significance, and frame of reference, signals of all sorts that the real teacher or preacher affirms who he/she was *and* is.

For those whose appearance or color differs from the target or audience group, it must be stated that such surface contrast is, at most, a temporary handicap. Deep rapport is possible across the vast variety of visual differences, provided the *sounds* are close to the hearer. The late Dr. E. L. Harrison of Washington, D.C., was as Caucasian in appearance as most White men, yet his fresh and stimulating interpretation of the gospel effectively reached thousands of Blacks. He was, along with many, the firm evidence that the ear image takes precedence over the eye image. When Whites protest their acceptance of Blacks and make that statement about "I never think of *you* as Black," they are saying, "I *hear* you as White." The deep reaches of language and culture can be colorblind, but not deaf. Even a president of the United States is much more vulnerable for having a corn pone accent than he would ever be for some slight visual deviation from standard or average. White-language Black newscasters and Black-tongued White disc jockeys all confirm the fact of the ear over the eye.

The most frequent question at this point is how one acquires a tongue that relates, when one simply does not have it naturally already. The answer is certainly not to be found in language lessons and vocal practice, intent on sitting where they sit, laudable as that may be. But one can definitely study other things that help one identify. Language is, along with vocabulary and accent, a repository of experience—an historical frame of reference. Those who would join a group or congregation must be familiar with their tradition and with the ways their history is reflected in the meanings of words and longer expressions. They who would sit with a group must also sit in equality, admiration, and sensitivity. One could say also "in humility," innocent of schemes to stake out a new expertise, write, and then sell books. Like Ezekiel, if one sits in their situation long enough, one understands. One also respects and admires their culture and personhood and, without rational decision, begins to avoid contrast in such cultural areas as dress and even speech. If one *never* sounds exactly like a native, one will still have shown such close identification as to be heard and understood, like Jesus of Nazareth in Judea, gladly.

A final question always arises concerning the use of the pulpit to unify people and culture. "Why not be a model of *one* culture and draw all persons together into that one?" Some go further and ask, "Why not use the pulpit to *lift* the people?" In response to the first question one could ask, "Which *one* culture would you draw them into?" The other question has already provided an answer, implying an objective of "helping" all members into standard culture, the tongue and style of the ruling class. Ironically, one should do just that. That is to say, the pulpit ought sufficiently to project standard culture so that no person in an economic or racial group or ghetto would miss receiving help to survive and deal in the world controlled by the majority. If the pulpit takes seriously the answering of Jesus' prayer for unity, this, also, is the least one can do to draw people into oneness. The fact is that there must be, however, a two-way street of mutual cultural enrichment, if there is to be true oneness and not merely absorption and psychic genocide.

For such a laudable goal, one cannot use influence that one does not have, and one has to win folks to a broader perspective from *inside* their own culture and speech community. A middle-class teacher cannot effectively invite an Appalachian pauper into mainstream American life when the two are separated by a bridgeless chasm, and the teacher speaks no Appalachian. Nor can a preacher invite persons to costly commitments and abundant living in the foreign speech of theological academia.

Even if the preacher fancies the priesthood of all believers to include fluency in academese, it will have to be *taught* in the existing tongue of the laity. Anytime a preacher cannot accomplish effective translation, it has to be from ignorance of one or the other of the tongues involved, if not from outright lack of understanding of the material being taught. That which one cannot interpret into the language and experience of the folk is not worth learning.

To speak with power one must sit where the people sit, experientially and culturally, ministering in priestly and prophetic ways from the inside of the group.

LANGUAGE AS HISTORICAL FRAME OF REFERENCE AND HERITAGE

Every language came into existence to record and interpret human experiences, so there could never be a single intimate American language of spiritual capacities (as opposed, for instance, to a language of trade) until there is a relatively uniform American *experience*. So long as subgroups have immeasurably contrasting histories, based on arbitrary barriers and divisions, there will continue to be widely differing subcultures and matching languages. The unity which is one goal of preaching has thus to cope with bridging gaps by means of crosscultural or intergroup interpretation of *experience*.

The 1976 hassle over Georgian Jimmy Carter's reference to himself as "born again" illustrates the huge difference a frame of reference can make. The South, America's Bible belt, has for years used this term to refer to an experience of grace not terribly different from a decisive religious experience anywhere in the United States. Southerners are quite comfortable with this term, and I have seen a whole political career launched on a "born again" lawyer's broadcast of his Sunday Bible class lesson. The North, on the other hand, has a much smaller group using the term, a religious segment associated with personal pietism and even with some religious fanaticism. This, combined with old stereotypes of Southern religious rationalization for slavery and lynching, gives the term the worst possible connotation among White Northerners, middle-class and above. Because of the suspicions raised, Carter's campaign had to engage in a major project of intergroup religious interpretations. Rather than to be angry or insensitive, Carter had to sit where his critics sat historically, and use language out of *their* frame of reference to explain his position.

Oddly enough Black religious leadership across the country had no such problems with Jimmy Carter's rebirth. The term is commonly used among the Black masses, and may even have had something to do with *gaining* their support of Carter. In the minds of many Blacks, this term out of the Bible (John 3:1–13) has no bad connotations because its other frame of reference is the Black church. The revivalism or evangelicalism which gave it to the Black church was strongest in the South, where most Blacks lived at the time it entered the culture. So, because Black and White shared this powerful root influence, Carter could easily communicate with Blacks. This is shared frame of reference and, of course, the sharing of the language that goes with it.

The image inventory that language represents varies from group to group, and most people will have more than one image connected with some words and phrases. The most effective images in matters of deep religion, however, will always come from the native culture and the longest and deepest experience. That is to say, persons repond most profoundly to the images of their earliest cultural formation—the folk concepts and language of the groups in which they were born. If they acquire more sophisticated terms and join a more prestigious group, the capacity for response to the earlier heritage is still greater, unless there is a violent revolt against that heritage, which is still response, even though negative. One could carry it still further and assert that no person makes his or her own God. The do-it-yourself deities inspire no trust and worship. If persons have visions of God when they are old, they are out of their folk inventory.

This is established beyond doubt when one deals with the dying. They never call up the *acquired* theories and images when

Black church on death

the real crunch comes. The approaching specter of death peels back the accretions of economic and intellectual upward mobility, and the *original person* walks stripped through the gate. What a tragedy that all but a small minority of Whites, many of whom are obscurantists, should largely avoid speaking to that original person in the profound, historic folk terms and frame of reference in which he/she is fluent!

In contrast with America's mainstream majority, the Black-culture image inventory and lingual heritage are at their best when dealing with the awesome topic of death. While White language gropes for euphemisms designed to disguise the reality, Black folk language abounds in direct and indirect reference. Of course, the corpus of images in the Spirituals gives no neat answers, but the world view faces the facts on a familiar basis and without horror. Its earlier African authors had been on "friendly terms with death,"[5] and thought of it as a partner with life, not an enemy. For Blackamericans this was not opposed to the biblical view of death as enemy (1 Cor. 15:26), since Paul was not referring to physical death, having stated (15:56) that the sting of death was sin. For Blacks, then, spirituals and sermons were laden with positive and low key references to death such as "one more river to cross."

There is profound Christian comfort in these simple folk images, even after proper consideration has been given to the fact that heaven could have meant, at times, simply freedom and/or escape from slavery.

Go down, death, easy, and bring my servant home.

Soon I will be done with the troubles of this world . . . going home to live with God. I'm going to see my mother . . .

We shall walk through the valley and shadow of death. We shall walk through the valley in peace.

Jesus gwine make my dyin' bed . . .

Going to put on my shoes and going to shout all over God's heaven . . .

The folk prayers of Black religion have the same view built into their language. Almost every petition by preacher, deacon, or "bench member" ends, *today,* with phrases such as this:

Now Lord, now Lord when I come to the end of my journey . . . *(or* When I've walked the last mile of the way . . .)

When this world can offer me a home no longer . . .

When, Lord, I'm done going out and coming in . . .

When we, like others, must go in to come out no more . . .

When I've sung my last song and prayed my last prayer . . .

When we've stacked hymn books and Bibles . . .

When we must stack our swords in the sands of time . . .

After this introduction to the prayer-ending topic of death, the request is made in many poetic ways for an easy departure and a happy home in eternity:

Meet me at the River Jordan, and cross me over in a calm tide . . .

Let me breathe my life out sweetly on thy breast . . .

Give us a home in your kingdom, where we shall praise thee throughout ceaseless ages . . .

Where the wicked shall cease from troublin', and the weary shall be at rest . . .

Let me hear your welcome voice saying, 'Well done, thou good and faithful servant, enter the joy . . .

Where every day will be Sunday, and Sabbath shall have no end . . .[6]

Spirituals had a celebrative quality dramatically combined with the most realistic of details:

Don't you hear those hammers still ringing? Surely he died on Calvary . . .

Were you there when they pierced Him in the side?

Thus embellished, and yet realistically portrayed, the affirmation of the inevitable end not only undergirded the positive reading of all of life, but served as a gentle goad for good living:

You better mind. . . . You got to give account at the judgment . . .

Before this time another year I may be dead and gone . . .

I want to be ready . . . to walk in Jerusalem just like John . . .

Just so you live, just so you die . . .

Needless to say, this brief sample of a huge inventory of folk images was employed also in the preaching, which likewise faced the final end with candor and strength. Black preachers also faced, and still face and affirm, the place of death in the scheme of things, partly because the world view and historical frame of reference are built right into the language to which they are accustomed. To use that folk language in preaching is to plug into a well-tested reservoir of deeply embedded insights, and, as already stated, a major strength of the best of the Black pulpit lies in its refusal to fight against deeply embedded culture—"primitive" wisdom from the centuries.

How, then, does this compare to the widely publicized trend of professional psychiatry to break the silence and face death squarely?[7] Dr. Elisabeth Kübler-Ross and others are manifestly correct in their healthy turn towards honestly facing death, but they have not been able to generate powerful images and symbolic tools for implementing this. Authentic ritual comes only from generations and even centuries of common experience, and this is possible only among supposedly "primitive" cultures, whose continuity has provided authentic adaptations, keeping their traditions intact and at the same time viable, sometimes even in twentieth-century urban America—Blackamerican religion/culture. The new findings about death, then, have raised a very valid issue, the cultural tools for the healing solution of which must come from another source than professional academia.

However, the churches and culture of middle-class America have some real possibilities in this task of candidly handling death. Kübler-Ross's work has only revealed a need, but the White-culture church may very well have the resources to take the task from there and find authentic images and terms capable of handling the topic of death. Although Black-american attitudes towards death came from Africa, the historic frame of reference from which Blacks drew most of their language and figures on the subject was early American evangelicalism. However much their quaint folk terms may seem unique to them today, the sharing of their roots with other groups still shows. This is particularly true of the more rigid and less poetic expressions of America's theologically conservative Christian family. Just as the hymn, "Amazing Grace," never really died among the general population, it seems reasonable to suppose that much of the beauty and strength that characterized Black-cultural tools for dealing with death is still buried somewhere in the common collective transconscious of main-stream America. And White scholars are grappling with the possibility of rediscovering and adapting these resources.[8]

I was launched on this suspicion of the commonality between Black and White roots over thirty years ago, by the comments of a White Northerner after a sermon I delivered before a largely Black congregation in the middle South. The text and sermon was summed up literally in the third stanza of the hymn "How Firm a Foundation:"[9]

> When through the deep waters I call thee to go,
> The rivers of woe shall not thee over-flow;
> For I will be with thee, thy troubles to bless,
> And sanctify to thee thy deepest distress.

The lady from the North just *loved* my use of the "quaint" word sanctify. She wondered where a Union Theological Seminary graduate would get his hands on such interesting relics, and if I had ever tried this sort of intelligent resurrection of a fossil of faith before. She was quite surprised when I told her that it wasn't a fossil in my world—it has been going strong continu-ously since long before I was born. The lady was shocked, but there was evidence that her roots were connected; she did respond to the religious resources for handling great grief which came out of the early American folk religious frame of reference. It was just that she or her parents had later acquired an intellectual objection or inhibition against some of the extremes of persons among whom such terminology continued to be used.

Despite the excesses of some, folk language has a way of clinging to such goodies as "sanctify," and to all the subtle wisdom and power that has been collected and funded from the common experience of the group that used or still uses such language. So long as the words are spoken by the group's descendants, some portion of that original image inventory will insist on surviving, despite the massive rational/intellectual attack of the scholarly establishment. The preacher who would tap this resource for redemptive contemporary ends needs only to join the life stream of the common folk, and interpret the gospel from that population base's heritage perspective.

This working from the residue of the tradition present is very important. Nevertheless, one of the worst mistakes one can make in dealing with a topic like death is to use religious images when persons have no background with which to understand them. The task of recovering preaching, then, includes the task of recovering and adapting a set of images and terms which will save and use the strengths of the experience pool and adapt to contemporary need. Just as one cannot preach in a biblical vacuum, so one cannot preach or even use language in a historical/cultural vacuum. One must either update the folk inventory, or try to baptize a whole new set of terms from other areas of experience; there are no other choices. I for one would far prefer updating language with tested strength (plus a few belated excesses) to trying to baptize words from completely different fields and trying to give them utterly new and ultimate-concern meanings.

LANGUAGE AS VOCABULARY

The preceding discussion of language as historical frame of reference has concluded in a discussion bordering on vocabulary exclusively, which is as it should be. However, vocabulary as such requires still further treatment, since there are factors controlling word choice which subdivide and elaborate a group's traditional stream of common experience. The most obvious in religious circles has to do with the language of the professionally educated staff person, as compared with the needs of mass lay-level understanding. We have already mentioned the obligation to translate all theological ideas into folk-type language. Terms from the word inventory of a person with a church vocation, no less than a doctor, a lawyer or an engineer, are *for a specialized audience.* They are no more appropriate for laity than German is for Georgians. The world of language is divided into vocabularies, also for regions, social groups or classes, age groups, and time periods. Even when a nation, for instance, has a shared historical frame of reference, such as was celebrated in the American Bicentennial, great pluralism and subgrouping occurs inside the freedom being celebrated.

The Clarence Jordan sermon at the end of chapter 5 provides excellent illustrations. The setting is subtly keyed to the Southern surroundings by the choice of magnolia trees and a regional beverage, the mint julep. Later on, the capacity of the story to reach the intended audience is further enhanced by use of the food vocabulary of the region. Fried chicken, black-eyed peas, gravy and collard greens would be heavenly eating for any typical citizen of Georgia, and the Heaven of the Parable is the more meaningful and desirable because of such regional details—words specific to their locality.

Words associated with contemporary living also enhance communication with the majority of listeners. The magnificent language of King James's version is unequaled for poetic purposes, but the details of a contemporary experience are best portrayed in contemporary language. The Roman Catholic use of Latin differs from the use of Elizabethan English only in the degree of remoteness. Dr. Jordan knew Greek well enough to earn his Ph.D. in the subject, but he gave no ancient Greek details (which might in some situations be very helpful) to interpret Abraham's speech about the impassibility of the gulf between Hell and Heaven (Luke 16:26). He simply talked about the breaking up of *traffic* both ways. Today's auto-oriented society needs no more to be said.

The same sort of contemporaneity is evident in Jordan's paraphrase of "Moses and the prophets," whom Abraham declares (Luke 16:29) the brothers yet living should hear more seriously. "They got the Baptist churches, . . . Methodist churches, . . . Presbyterian churches, . . . Episcopalian churches, . . . preachers, . . . Bible. . . ." Moses and the prophets may not mean much to the modern mind, but the Baptists and the Methodists are right here before one's eyes, and altogether understandable as representatives of contemporary religion.

Of course there may be objections from some to the fact that Jordan used the word *got* for *have* four times in one section. That is because *got* is used for the present tense of *have* only by people who are low-brow—poor and/or ignorant and untrained. The word *ain't* is in the same general category, but these words do not tarnish Jordan in the least. Only a fool would think he used them in ignorance. Sensitive spirits know immediately that Jordan is drawing close to certain people. Just how much this linguistic closeness can mean may vary, but for some it means a great deal. The fact is that they themselves often know full well that what they are saying is not "proper," but their identity with their group overrules their ambitions to seem part of more respected groups, higher on the totem pole. And they respond deeply to a preacher who parallels Jesus' risky fellowship with publicans and sinners.

The young of all classes respond in much the same way when their special vocabulary, not yet recognized as proper, is used in a sermon. Some call it slang, but a few words like *dig* (for understand), *way out* (approval), *bread* (money), *cat* (male person), and *fuzz* (police) used naturally in meaningful discourse have gained immeasurable rapport with many teenagers. Gray hair means nothing if one speaks their tongue authentically. Again, the ear takes precedence over the eye.

Jordan employs one *high-brow* colloquialism with similarly subtle and telling effect. When the rich man in Hell is made to cry in typical Southern aristocratic arrogance, "Boy! bring me some water!" a world of prophetic judgment on the formerly rigid class structures of the South is expressed. Little wonder that Jordan's Americus, Georgia, project was constantly in danger of being burned out. The powerful implications of such renditions as this were hard to miss.

Deep feeling, also, is often well expressed in local and low-class terms. When the rich man is made to suggest, in Jordan's version that "Lazarus go back and kinda scare the daylights out of them," one gets the picture quite clearly, and one has the feelings to match. The delivery helped, of course, but without such vocabulary the delivery would have been out of character.

One final word about language as vocabulary concerns the impermanence of the ratings. When I referred to the private language of the teenagers as "not yet recognized as proper," I was simply and naturally alluding to the fact that most new words begin as "slang." The same is true of many supposedly ungrammatical usages. *Ain't* will probably not always be classified as colloquial, dialectal and substandard. Status goes up as usage increases. Language is dynamic, and usage makes acceptance. The sentences I start with *and* were forbidden when I was a boy, but functionality and wide usage have changed all that. The preacher who uses any language at all should be humbly aware that the only eternal vocabulary is in heaven. Down here we are understood by means of the signal system that prevails in the speech communities wherein we preach, at the time *when* we preach.

LANGUAGE AS DIALECT

The Jordan sermon also illustrates to the ear the issue of language as dialect. The recorded rendition was all in a pleasant Georgia drawl. The learned storyteller made no effort whatever to identify with the larger world of standard, mass-media English pronunciation. He was in popular demand all over our country as lecturer and preacher, perhaps in spite of and not because of his accent. Or else his light so shown that people saw his tremendous good works and respected his total identification with his multiracial witness in a benighted area of bigotry. How important, then, is dialect in communication?

Quite obviously dialect is important when a Cockney or a Brooklynite cannot be understood in Peoria. It hurts me to remember how little I understood of Paul Tillich's German-accent English in his classes in the early 1940s. Scotch accents are more prestigious in the preaching industry, but people who are not accustomed to a heavy burr can never relax enough to hear and experience the word event properly. They are too busy trying simply to get a clear verbal signal.

Dialects also signal identity. The Brooklynese of the Bible tale to juveniles in chapter 5 drew a few backfires because two or three boys associated the accent with big-time crime and racketeers. The brother of the speaker was asked, "How come you're such a gentleman and your brother is such a hood?" He was a recent ex-Brooklynite, but his audience was not; and that was a mistake for a multilingual story teller. If dialects can be consciously chosen, one should always avoid projecting a questionable image. The fact is, of course, that *no* dialect is useful for preaching save that of the hearers. If the audience accent is not natural to the speaker, her or his own native tongue is far the best replacement.

The dialect of any group is only the result of an accepted inventory of sounds. If the group is in America but comes from elsewhere, the sound inventory of the country of origin will continue, even though applied to a new language. Former Secretary of State Kissinger is a prominent example. The dialect of the West African and West Indian Black is another, combining an African "phoneme inventory," as they are called, with an English "lexical inventory" or vocabulary. As has already been implied, this repertoire of vocal elements (out of which words are made) can best be altered by an all-out identification with the new speech community, issuing in a habitual and intuitive effort to avoid contrast. Thus the failure of a Puerto Rican child to speak standard English may not mean at all that the child has low intelligence. Rather it may reflect that he or she is happily and primarily identified with Spanish-speaking parents and other significant persons in a self-sufficient speech community. The thing to remember is the fact that standard English is only the dialect of the middle class of mid-America, which happens also to be used in television and radio.

The dynamics of dialect are very deep and no hard and fast rules may be advanced. Suffice it to say that a sensitive person with a sensitive ear will avoid many subtly generated misunderstandings in a new speech community. Also, the change of a few nuances of sound may be adequate to say, at least part of the time, like J. F. Kennedy, *"Ich bin ein Berliner."* A sound here and there can help one say, "I am *one* with you, even though I dare not to pretend to be one of you."

CONCLUSION

The conclusion of the matter of preaching as folk language is that there are many different folks even in one congregation, and that preachers must learn, with Paul, that they are made all things to all men, that they might by all means save some (1 Cor. 9:22). Whenever possible, one ought to use the language pattern of the majority of an audience, but no smaller segment can be linguistically ignored with impunity. Such elements as America's folk religious heritage of revivalism will vary, also, from region to region, but the influence has not disappeared from the collective transconsciousness of any regional group. Academic judgmentalism has purged hymn books of folk favorites such as "Amazing Grace," but they will not be utterly destroyed. The historic frame of reference is still a part of the language, influencing religion and politics and all of life. They who would preach with power, must recover the power of the traditional folk-language resources for dealing with life and death, while at the same time adapting that great reservoir to serve this present age. Thus will the gospel reach the unvarnished and real inner person—the elemental transconsciousness of all classes and ages which yearns beneath the acquired exteriors of a humanity which is slowly choking to death spiritually.

7. Preaching as Dialogue

To ACHIEVE vital experience with transconscious impact, preaching demands participation. Proclamation with power requires dialogue. Folk culture, folk/biblical heritage and folk language must be expressed in a fully folk-type medium. The whole tribe or extended family not only confers authority on their cultic birthright; they take decisive part in it, both in its regular rendition at various ritual occasions and in the informal process of passing it on from generation to generation. More sophisticated structures of religion proclaim the priesthood of all believers, suggesting comparably broad grounds for the inclusion of all members of a community in any process as central to their worship as preaching is to Protestants. The reasons for thinking of preaching as dialogue are, thus, many and varied. In a summary in keeping with the approach of this work, it might be said that the contemporary goal of an oral tradition of biblical religion, held dear by persons as individuals and in community, must be achieved and confirmed in the expression/witness of all worshipers, in preaching, as well as in the work of the church. Preaching cannot be the private province of an elite priesthood, even though that professional body must do much to make the Word/experience worthy of the title Gospel. Persons learn and grow because of involvement far better than they do from detached and inert attention. Ritual and various other forms of dialogue offer much in this vein toward the recovery of preaching.

This is a terribly abstract way to introduce so lively a topic as preaching dialogue, so now a more concrete definition is in order. The word dialogue is used here to denote the pulpit/pew context of spontaneous interaction, which may be audible or silent—involving physical or body language and/or mental response. Whatever the form, the communicating and responding are genuine. Unlike Plato's *Dialogues,* where imaginary conversations were written by an elite genius, dialogue here is unwritten and unrehearsed, except as cultural expectations have a way of generating repetition of meaningful communications. The range of dialogic possibilities is very wide, but whatever the culture permits or demands must issue in authentic, meaningful, and mutual exchange of convictions—thoughts and feelings—between pulpit and pew.

THE BLACK TRADITION OF DIALOGUE

Because exposure to pulpit dialogue is so limited among Americans generally, a practical illustration of the phenomenon may be more possible, as well as more appropriate than a definition as such. The best-known and perhaps the most authentic practice of pulpit/pew dialogue in America today is found in the worship of the Black masses. It is still very common to encounter lively exchange between preacher and people, full of conviction, joy and freedom. Indeed, if such is not the case, the church is not a church of the Black masses—almost by definition. Thus, among Blacks, it has been interesting to listen to all the "new" White ideas about preaching as dialogue, when they have had call-and-response in Africa for centuries, and in Black Christian worship in America from the very start—three centuries ago. The dialogic method has been completely "road-tested" in Black culture, approved, and given permanent place. It includes responses from the pew which range all the way from brief bursts of affirmation (Amen! Sho' 'nough! Yes sir! So true! etc.), to culturally choreographed counterpoint, with the preacher's intoned Gospel cast in a continuous context of congregational chant ("The Lord is My Shepherd, and I Shall Not Want" or "Lord, Have Mercy . . . on my Soul" or "Bread of Heaven, Bread of Heaven, Feed me till I want no more" may be the lyrics of this chanted background, but in every case they are less important than the musical setting and support which they provide. I find it literally impossible to preach in such a context without my own matching intonation, in the same key).

In addition to affirmations of agreement, one hears coaching as well. If a point is especially new or needed, one may be encouraged to "Stay right there." Or if one has presumably taught long and well, and the hearer thinks it is time to climax and celebrate, the word heard is, "Come on up!" One may even be asked to hush, because the ecstasy of hearing is more than the listener can bear. Or the hearing may be interrupted by an irrepressible shout. Whatever the form of the dialogue, the Black worshiper feels authorized to express her/himself, with the result that the sermon is always a dialogue. Even Black silence in such churches is a loud and clear indication of poor preaching or of poor relations with the congregation.

Of course, not all the hearers respond verbally; indeed only a small minority in most congregations give the audible responses. However, they speak *for* the less expressive as well as for themselves, and very few of the more inhibited would wish the entire audience to be as silent as they. Smiles and other facial expressions, nodding of the head, intensity of gaze, and edge-of-the-seat position all contribute to the communication between preacher and people. And dialogue doesn't stop with the formal end of a sermon. Nor does the "Amen Corner" have a monopoly on being heard. After a recent revival sermon on the justice of God, and after the offering as well, a person rose to say what the sermon meant in her life as a State College employee. She had never testified in all her life, but the tradition was so prevalent that she had no qualms about adding her two minutes at a rather late hour.

It is also true that not all of a sermon is equally prone to draw affirmative response. Three of the most likely reasons are the type of material, the cues given by the speaker, and the stage of progress towards the climax. Thought-provoking preachment requires intense thought; it is hard to talk and think at the same time. Noncelebrative narrative material will usually keep listeners busy experiencing the story. Apart from the outbursts of delight or horror one might hear at a good movie, Black preaching audiences are occupied with the enjoyment of the story. Silence, therefore, is not uniformly a signal of poor impact. It may simply be inappropriate or not very handy to engage in dialogue. Indeed, a story is not normally thought of in quite the same dialogic terms.

On cue, however, audible response can be elicited at almost any time except the periods of absorption in the action of a story. There are traditional requests for feed-back, easily understood pauses in rhythmic address which call for response, and code words to which echo is traditionally given. The direct request or candid appeal for the audience's support in the preaching struggle may take a variety of forms: "Are you praying with me?" "You're getting mighty quiet out there." "Can I get an Amen?" or "Help me, Jesus!" Again, there is a style of Black preaching which is done in short, rhythmic phrases, between which space is given for response. The purpose is well and widely understood, and members of my preaching classes often criticize each other for failing to pause long enough to let the people have their part. And, finally, there are words which are known as signals or calls for an echo of affirmation. *Surely* is such a word, as in "Surely goodness and mercy shall follow me all the days of my life" (Ps. 23). *Truly* is used interchangeably with *surely* in such passages as "Truly this was the Son of God" (Matt. 27:54).

The very common, "Mercy, Lord!" always draws another "Mercy" from the audience, and almost any one or two-syllable word projected and repeated will be perceived as a calling for response, supportive of the preacher and fulfilling of the responder, as mentioned in chapter 4 on celebration.

The incidence of audible responses increases as the pitch and intensity rise towards the climax of a Black sermon. Authentic reply is not perfunctory or routine; it arises irrepressibly out of celebration. The impact of great truth coupled with deep experience is heightened and made unforgettable by the very fact that one has joined transconsciously in affirming and celebrating it.

Two questions arise in the face of such a description: Why is it so different; and, Why has it no parallel in the culture of the majority, if it is so beautifully moving and effective?

For some the question is false. Southern-culture Whites of lower socioeconomic classes and many Pentecostals from all over America engage in variations on the same theme. In rebuttal, one could deal with tremendous differences, not all of them subtle, between Black and White patterns of response. However, it is far more profitable to view the two racial traditions in historical perspective, and to be aware of the strong possibility that this similarity is the first fruits of a more serious two-way exchange between White and Black religious traditions. Whites of the early American revival had enough Amens to encourage Africans to come to the surface with their call-and-response patterns and know that this would be acceptable in Christian worship. The Whites, in turn, were deeply influenced by the fervor and freedom of Black response. On balance, as I have said already,[1] Black culture influenced White at least as much as White influenced Black at this point, and probably a great deal more. Three things are certain: a majority of Blacks of all classes still embrace preaching dialogue and give it the acceptance which middle-class Whites give in theory but not in practice; the whole Pentecost movement grew out of a Black revival where dialogue was constantly evident; and the emergence of racial and cultural self-awareness among very gifted Blacks is establishing a much more widely understood rationale for this important aspect of worship.

To return to the reasons for Black and White difference, then, one must start with the African roots of Black religion. During a much publicized *durbar* (reception, including traditional welcome addresses) given at Cormantin, Ghana,[2] for the Martin Luther King Program, I heard long praise speeches in honor of the King Program Fellows, and myself as head of this "state." But the most memorable part will always be the call and response—the pauses in the Chief's oratorical flights when the whole group cried "Yo!" It was their way of saying Amen! Their warmth of welcome was most moving, but they sounded so much like Black deacons from Stateside, that all our souls were deeply stirred in a ritual of sudden self-recognition. We knew as never before that we were deeply African, no matter how long our stock had been removed or how much it had been mixed. The way we do dialogue is not a poor attempt at duplicating White patterns long since dead in mainline denominations, but a beautiful folk phenomenon which expresses and confirms and teaches and helps preachers, after the manner of our African ancestors.

The pattern of Black preaching dialogue has remained virtually unchanged because of cultural/religious isolation, in which for generations, 11:00 A.M. on Sundays has been America's most segregated hour. That same widespread discrimination against Blacks has kept them from other opportunities throughout American life, and this has left the Black church in far the most important place in ghetto life. Thus, for purposes of expression, to take a speaking part in the crucial rite of preaching has been a privilege to be welcomed, and at times, all too eagerly sought. With cultural roots that may be thousands of years old, coupled with preservative isolation and preaching themes that are relevantly prone to beget response, the practice of dialogue in Black preaching is likely to continue to be alive and well in the ghetto for many generations yet to come. When the differences with White culture are finally dissolved, this is one place in the two-way cultural exchange where Black culture is likely to give much more than it receives.

However, it is a human process, and quite a distance from being uniformly perfect. The too-eager participants just mentioned are well known. Many Blacks have been outspoken in their criticism of this group, thinking of them as being false and in the majority. The critics are quite correct in suggesting a combination of conditioned response and downright manipulation. This is often perpetrated by preachers fluent in the culture, but the laity are no less manipulative in their expansion or contraction of dialogue, according to their likes or dislikes of the speaker. Just a few whispering priests turned the crowd's cry to "Crucify him!" and a few key deacons or denizens of the Amen Corner can turn a Black congregation against the best of preachers. Overly sympathetic laity have been known, also, to overstimulate a preacher and "nearly preach him to death," throwing his timing off and requiring that he rise to a climax from a plane already established much too high.

A more general and profound criticism comes from Vernon Johns, perhaps the most seminal Black American preacher-theologian of the twentieth century. Mentioned in my *Black Preaching*,[3] it suggests that the culture as a whole is prone to generate great enthusiasm which issues in the immediate need to *do* something. People "holler" about it in affirmative dialogue, and think that they have been discharged from all further obligations. Some preachers, no less under illusion, consider their obligations fulfilled when they have delivered a stirring message, without any follow-through or implementation whatsoever.

However, Dr. Johns, himself, was equally critical of cold, unresponsive religious worship. And his brilliant successor at the Dexter Avenue Baptist Church of Montgomery, Alabama, Martin Luther King, Jr., was modern America's most activist preacher, not in spite of his dialogue with Black masses, but *because* of it. The "I Have a Dream" speech was in fact a sermon, which drew dialogue from hundreds of thousands, roaring across America on television, but also moving the Civil Rights cause forward by giant steps on many fronts. One dare not throw out the baby with the bath. One does not have to stop there just because preaching dialogue is so ecstatically fulfilling, affirming the responsive hearer as well as the speaker and the truth uttered.

Dialogue also gets people on the record for Christian conviction, and for the causes affirmed, while getting into their own personal record and memory the unparalleled retention of that truth affirmed and the commitment to it.

However, the reenforcement given is not all for the audience alone. Dialogue is a most freeing and fulfilling factor for the preacher during the sermon. Not only is it *easier* to preach in authentic dialogue; the *quality* goes up. No Black preacher I have ever met has denied the tremendous value of authentic dialogue. There has been mention of overreaction and usurpation of services, when people virtually took over, and the preacher couldn't be heard, but this is not real dialogue. This is more of a listener's ego trip, issuing in a contest with the speaker. Such extremes aside, it can easily be declared that without dialogue, there is no distinctively Black sermon, it is just that crucial to Black preaching.

Dr. Sandy F. Ray casually and comically stated the case unforgettably well:

> He (a White Southern Baptist minister) said to me, "Sandy, I know you can preach. You can preach *any*where, and we want to hear you preach like you preach in *your* church."
>
> I said, "I don't think I can do that."
>
> "Don't you bother about us. You just preach the gospel."
>
> That's just like asking a doctor to perform a major operation, when he only has his bag with him. If he's going to perform a major operation he has to have all his equipment. He has to be in a hospital where he has all the nurses, all the other attending doctors, and an operating room. You can't have a major operation just with a bag." If you want me to preach like I preach at home, you have to have somebody to say at the proper place, "Come on up!"
>
> They were very nice to me *after* I preached. But when I played baseball, I wanted people to cheer me when I was playin'. I didn't need them after the game was over.[4]

Thousands of Black preachers would heartily join me in concurring with this appraisal of the importance of dialogue in the Black tradition. When one of my own deacons once asked me why I hadn't preached in our home church like I preached in a small church in the midst of the cotton fields near Lemoore,

California, I simply replied "Y'all doesn't he'p me like they did."

WIDER SIGNIFICANCE

I have yet to meet a White preacher who is any less enthusiastic than Black about the salutary effects of Black dialogue on his preaching. One went so far as to state that he would be a much better preacher—maybe even a great one— with "that kind of help every Sunday." The analytic details are not easy to isolate; in fact the reasons for the White preacher's response to Black audience dialogue are as unpredictable as Jesus declared the renewal of the Holy Spirit to be (John 3:8). Yet there are obviously cultural and other factors among Blacks which create a more inviting preaching climate than other contexts for presumably stimulating and creative spiritual interaction. Even though exact duplication is impossible with White audiences, surely there are some guidelines which should increase this needed contextual influence on the White pulpit.

Before attempting to spell out the Black-culture inputs potentially applicable to White preaching dialogue, it must be wondered out loud why such a process has not occurred much sooner and on a wider scale. The testimony of White preachers about Black audiences is at least fifty years old to my own knowledge. As a small child I heard two different famous White preachers, the kind who were in national demand, declaring the joys and benefits of the Black audience. Their gratitude was doubled at that time, because they couldn't invite the Black host pastor into their own pulpits for return engagements. Yet none of the many White witnesses to the value of Black-style dialogue seemed ever to have made any serious attempt to capture the magic and make it work in the White church. It is more than passing strange that seminary curricula and other places of preacher training and renewal have ignored this gold mine until very recently.

The answer to this question is essential, since whatever prevented exchange historically is inescapably still present to some extent. The issue is then not subtle vengeance by dangling the skeletons from the preacher's closet; rather it is the realistic facing and conquering of emotional and other blocks which have operated as much in certain classes of Blacks as among the vast majority of Whites.

In a fashion quite parallel to the already mentioned social-class indicators associated with language strata, audible dialogue has been associated with "primitive" religion. A few elite scholarly types have learned to identify the subtle benefits unseen by the culturally biased eye, but everybody else, including most of the "primitives" themselves, looks down on the ancient culture, and, of course, on the low socioeconomic status of its practitioners in this country. How often have marvelously warm Black worshipers publicly apologized to bodies of White visitors, "You'll have to excuse us. We haven't learned to worship quiet and dignified like yet." Within the last ten years a Black seminary president informed me that his students would learn these primitive patterns all too soon in "the street," after graduation. He was not about to pollute his curriculum with any serious consideration of such. Attitudes like this are so widespread because the world view of Western society is dichotomized into flesh-and-spirit, with body and emotion excluded from the holy of holies. Modern psychiatry and sensitivity training are busy trying to put people back in touch with their bodies, but religion tends to resist this wholeness even while preaching it. Black dialogue is a road-tested, authentic cultural tool which comes out of the distant past, but copes effectively with present needs. It may be a part of the providential antidote for the Greek dualism which has plagued Euro-American culture from the beginning of its supposed civilization.

The issue of dialogue viewed in these terms, can be faced squarely. When the irrationally resistant sectors of the trans-conscious signal a retreat from the raucous reverence of real people, the courage to persist has reasonable foundation. It can be based not on a romantic, "liberal" attachment to those quaint and oppressed Blacks, but on a sense of desperate personal need, spelled out in Western clinical terms, as well as in the statistics of a dying church.

TOWARDS DIALOGUE

The foregoing rationale requires an orderly process of acculturation, if inhibited congregations of any race are to move towards dialogue, or to return to it. I have a doctoral student whose dissertation is completely devoted to developing a sound (not overly threatening) process to help a Black middle-class congregation "come home culturally," and serve its neighborhood constituency better. The word acculturation is very important, since the sectors of the transconscious where the related meanings and responses are stored are not amenable to exclusively rational argument. These responses were formed over a period of generations, on the basis of data not reasoned out in the first place. It was status fears and strivings for upward mobility—wholesome ambition and motivation for progress—which was twisted to form these sick inhibitions. Fussing and argument about the matter only vent the hostilities of the preacher who may have been fortunate enough to get a little bit ahead of the members in the journey back to wholeness. The Black Methodist I heard angrily asking why his congregation didn't say "Amen" was only confirming their image of dialogue as uncouth. Acculturation takes reason and sensitivity and time, so that change is not bought with the price of healthy self-respect. For we are our feelings and cultural orientation, as well as our reasoned thoughts; and our *highest* religious instincts are already beyond reason, drawing us to God even when reason would doubt or deny.

How does one launch a process of acculturation, designed to impact and substantially alter the less rational sector of the transconscious? How does one implement these insights about dialogue? Ten attitudinal changes or guidelines are offered here for movement toward a recovery of dialogue. This is followed by a plan, the beginnings of a concrete program of implementation.

First, dialogue is *personal*. All forms of response, audible or not, must be understood not as the liturgical obligation of proper worshipers, but the personal response of the hearer to the preacher. Of course this automatically eliminates the *formal* speech-sermon, since personal response cannot properly be given to impersonal address. No matter how many limitations to intimacy are obvious in the setting of mass worship, the primary character of the communication-event is personal. There is no question about this in the culture of the Black masses, since the preacher is a literal and intimate "father" in the extended-family congregation. White culture must maintain wholesome professional respect and expectation of the strictest professional preparation and ethics, but professional *distance* is contrary to the very Kingdom of God, where there is neither Jew nor Greek, bond nor free, male nor female (Gal. 3:28).

It follows that the pastor-member *personal relation is characterized by concern*. The hired professional, even, is worthy of certain employee or contractual benefits, but the parson/person is worthy of more individual and intimate concern. Likewise, even the patient or client of the professional deserves certain caring services, but the "kin" person in Christ is worthy of much more, expressed not alone in the pulpit communication, but at all times and in all kinds of need. A few years ago I was asked to advise army chaplains from around the world concerning ministry to Blacks. The point of the subsequently published presentation[5] was that no chaplain can fail to risk his neck for the welfare of his Black troops and expect them to show up for a sermon on Sunday. The Army had to face this and compensate for bad chaplain's ratings by local commanding officers, when that low rating resulted from advocacy against the residual racist injustices which still dog the Black foot soldier. I have since come to see that the case of the "bench-member" is little different from that of the enlisted man. The big contrast is that while the chief of chaplains had to change rating procedures, the Lord of the universe had long since announced the caring pastor's standing: "Inasmuch as you did it unto the least of these . . . " (Matt. 25:40).

Dialogue between caring persons ta<u>kes place by means of *a</u> *variety of signals and responses, audible and inaudible*. The lively audibles of Black dialogue may not be nearly half of the total communication which goes out from the audience, as much as I love personally to hear response. It is far more important to be able to sense that persons are free to engage in verbal and other heard expression than it is that this freedom should be exercised continually. The totally silent Black church is trying not to be related to the Black masses, but the perpetually noisy Black congregation may have problems just as serious. The point is that too little has been made of the silent responses of persons in dialogue in all cultural groups.

The signals of body language are far more important than we usually are rationally aware. We perceive tension in the shoulders of a speaker or hearer, and we respond without rational decision. The set of a jaw, the hang of a hand, or the cross of a leg bespeak a great deal. All this before one even starts to deal with the more obviously legible facial expressions. Auditoriums are sensed to be alive and stimulating, although silent, because a speaker responds transconsciously to the forward-leaning posture of an expectant audience. One needs no training to know how enthusiastic they feel, or to be aware of their boredom, if that happens to be the case.

<u>Body language reflects attitude</u>s—the thinking and feeling response of hearers. It may be more accurately indicative of dialogue than the sincere but sometimes independent shouting of a person whose release in the spirit comes with the supportive presence of the congregation, with or without a sermon—to say nothing of the insincere Amens which are given routinely. Most Blacks have seen a deacon or other functionary who awoke from a sound sleep to cry "Amen!" If it was sincere, it was in a terribly different dialogue; it was saying to the congregation, "See, I am awake!" I remember with deep gratitude a row of "young" deacons (late thirties to early fifties) whose arm movement silently attested to the fact that their cups were running over, and they had to dry the tears. No matter how much I may love audible dialogue, the genuine and deep exchange with those

largely silent deacons will always be one of my most treasured memories of dialogue.

Whatever way persons respond, their best *participation in dialogue is based on their sense of needs met*. The preacher who would draw congregations into meaningful interaction must address their vital concerns. All other means of eliciting response are audience manipulation. Great charisma is based on style and genius, to be sure, but the genius that moves great crowds is employed in the meeting of *their needs* as they see them. Martin Luther King, Jr., had such charisma; the response to his preaching was not only heard in rising dialogue, but seen in the later commitment of hundreds and perhaps thousands who joined him in dangerous demonstrations for justice, accepting brutality and prison willingly. However, Dr. King's magnificent style and dazzling genius would have meant less than nothing if they had not been dedicated to what Black millions perceived as a need to be free. In the exact same area of the country, uncouth bigots, who saw no such need and opposed Black liberation, scoffed at his genius and called him "Martin Luther Coon." Conversations with congregations have to be about things they are deeply interested in—things so pressing they forget formalities and are caught up in the discussions.

It is this same choice of topics of need which is referred to in chapter 3 as the "Great Themes" on which preaching's meaningful experiences must be based. Meaning*less*ness is inevitable when topics are chosen for their cleverness, forgetting the people's plight in a bid for glory. Even intense response may be meaningless if centered around a sensitive but already outworn topic. Many a graveyard climax to a Black sermon falls under this judgment, and even the ever-effective story of one's conversion borders on it if not substantially varied in focus each time it is used. It is far better to bet one's preaching reputation on need than on gimmicks of style and the traditional soft places where the audience's emotions are easily reached. The great themes of human need live up to the command to feed the sheep, and God honors the efforts in ways that are all the more satisfying because they were not planned or predictable.

I saw this as never before when I preached recently on "The Guidance of God," in a church where I was known, but not as a great preacher. Frankly, audience expectations were very low. The topic, when dealt with honestly, was no help either, since it was complicated and difficult. Yet from the beginning the audience rapport was very good. My 20/20 hindsight would seem now to suggest that this was almost exclusively due to a felt need on part of the congregation to know better how to find and know God's will and guidance. The final illustration was taken from Margaret Walker's magnificent novel of the Civil War and reconstruction period, *Jubilee*. It was the story of Vyrie's dilemma as she faced two living, legal husbands. The first, long presumed dead in the Civil War, had suddenly appeared, to protect and offer education to his two children, born when his wife Vyrie was still a slave. The second husband was a hardworking, faithful dirt farmer, and loving husband and father to her third child. He had also cared well for the first two children. The first husband was rich, literate, handsome and devoted. He would send his children to college and make Vyrie much more comfortable. He certainly had prior claim on her, legally speaking. The second husband loved the Lord and loved his wife and family—and worked hard to make crops. How do you choose in a case like that? As the story closed with Vyrie's guidance from God, and the sermon closed with a prayer for guidance, the dialogue with the congregation was rich and meaningful; there was authentic shouting and widespread verbal response. Because some of the most audible participation came from persons who had never been heard before, I could not help thinking that there was a Vyrie or two right in the audience, and their joyful participation was from the guidance which they had received for their own parallel needs.

Here was urgent personal need stated and answered in *familiar terms*—almost too familiar, so intense was the response. It is the intuitively generated emphasis on such needs and on such intimately familiar images and terms which gives some unlettered preachers their great drawing power, while the formally trained languish in relative obscurity. Education for ministry must develop a whole new strategy for sensitivity to those needs and fluencies in the signal system of the folk to whom one wishes to preach.

However, more important, even, than the language heritage are the traditional objects of trust. *Dialogue is built on shared certainties.* People are not fed by the open-ended discussion; their needs are not served by unanswered advancement of cute questions. They demand always something new and fresh, but they want it to relate to something in which they have equity and involvement. Dialogue occurs best when folks have some notion that a familiar field of faith is to be covered, and when they can help press on to a fresher and deeper understanding and gut relationship to it. Audiences should be involved in the decision-making process, after stimulating questions are raised. But there has to be some formal acquaintance with the topic— some previous certainty on which to build the shared solution.

In the Black world, no certainty is more shared than the Providence of God. After writing about it for years, I finally got around to preaching about it several times. The effect of the shared quality of dialogue was uniformly electric, even though some of these ideas were as much out of John Calvin as out of the biblical and traditional African heritages. The closing illustration-narrative was from Genesis 50:15–21, Joseph's speech to his brother. Through the first part of the story, where nobody knew what this had to do with Providence, there was a silent suspense. But just as soon as they saw how this related to the original text of Romans 8:28 and the commonly shared certainties of providence, the whole audience joined in to finish up the answer and celebrate a new view of an old certainty:

> If you want to know from somebody way back yonder how God works, ask Joseph.
> They had been to bury his father at Machpelah, and they had come back to Egypt to their wives and their flocks, and their families whom they had left there. They were settling down now. Daddy, the great patriarch, was gone, And once he was gone there was a whole new set of relations in the family, because fathers was very impor-
> tant people then, and when the father left somebody had to decide

now who was the new Daddy. Well, some interesting problems arose at that point.

Father Jacob had anticipated all this, and so he had advised his other sons and forewarned them. So they on the advice of their father came before Joseph with a speech that went something like this:

Brother, we sold you into slavery, and somehow you stayed a nice person. You went through that trick bag with Potiphar's wife and you kept your cool, and somehow you didn't get bitter about it. You did time in Pharaoh's prison, but you gave your stretch in that big-house a spiritual purpose, and you came out of there also without bitterness. After that you made good in the Government, and that didn't turn your head either.—When we turned to you for food in that big shortage, you treated us just wonderful. But now, here's nitty-gritty, we think Daddy was probably right. You were nice to us because of respect for him, and now he's *gone!* And we're on our own, and we feel like chickens running from a hawk in an open field. There ain't *no* place to hide! It's only a matter of time till you git us, either out in the open or some way under cover. And we've come up here together to ask you to forgive us. *Please,* we're willin' to be your servant; we're willin' to do *any*thing; we put ourselves at your mercy; we crawl at your feet. *Please,* Sir! Please, little brother, have mercy on us!

Joseph had been crying almost from the start, and he raised his hand and wiped his eyes, and when he could get hisself together and get his feelings to where he could speak intelligibly, he said, "Don't be scared. Do you think I'm in God's place? Do you think I'd try to get the vengeance that only God is supposed to have? I'm no God. Lookee here, I know what happened. I know you meant to do me in. I know you were jealous of me and Dad, and hatred between brothers is the worse kind of hatred there is. And I know you were evil to the core, or you never could of thrown your own brother into slavery. But I also know my God, and I know how he works. I know he'll never let your enemies go but so far, and I know he'll always make sure his children have enough left of what it takes to make it. And I know that if I wait on him and serve his purposes, and try to live by his will, he's gonna make it come out alright. I know for myself that he reserves the right to make everything come out like *He* wants it to come out. *You meant it to me for evil, but God meant it to me for good!*

Certainty as enthusiastic as that of the preacher and people in this case has drawn a lot of criticisms in recent generations, because mainline conservative White Christianity has been loaded with aggression and overdone. It has also been quite often negative rather than positive. However, as I have stated often, Black tradition is fiery—but fiery *glad* rather than mad. Fire or intensity of *certainty begets dialogue only if warmth is relaxed*. There is calmness about genuine assurance which shuns meeting the congregation more than halfway. The preacher sets the table, but doesn't try to *force* folk to eat. Overwhelming presentation squelches people's animation. There has to be a happy balance between undersell and overkill.

Overkill not only squelches dialogue; it insults people as well. Every lawyer is taught to press facts only so far. Beyond that the very pressure suggests, "I know you to be a fool, so I am doing all I can to penetrate the density of your ignorance." To be sure, of course, there are congregations which accept preachers in this vein, but they are unhealthily programmed to believe that they are, in fact, nobodies who need to be yelled at. Their response on cue must never be mistaken for responsible dialogue. Authentic conversation between preacher and people should be at least as animated as any other conversation, but the certainties shared are never tainted with hidden aggression. And the speaker's warmth is designed to kindle warmth in the hearers rather than to overwhelm or smother their fires. As almost every great Black preacher says from time to time, "I don't know about you, but I . . . "

This is another way of saying that *genuine respect for the hearer is essential to preaching dialogue.* This means that one is not only permissive concerning the form that the hearer's response will take; one is prepared to accept a contrasting opinion. The moment a preacher perceives all critics to be devils incarnate, the process of dialogue comes to a screeching halt. Conversation cannot be preplanned; if people are not free, there is no real exchange. Dogmatism is another form of the ferocity just mentioned, and it leaves no room for discussion. One of the most important things a preacher can do to encourage dialogue is to practice personally and project generally a supportive and permissive attitude towards all types and stripes.

Spectatorism in liturgy has many causes, but one reason for the demise of dialogue has surely been the elitist attitude of professional clergy who were bent on "proper" services. They have clearly projected the idea that in so demanding a setting, members are to be seen and not heard—except when called upon. It may be that the most healing facet in all Black worship is the reverence held for every single person's right to religious expression. A participant has to go to unusual lengths to be silenced in a service. When *respect for people takes precedence over the status associated with being correct,* the dialogue can begin. And the church where persons are respected and their needs met can anticipate participation which goes far beyond spectatorism both in worship and in the world.

Finally, *dialogue demands discipline.* Just as sermon preparation has to hold up and pursue a single purpose, there must be an exercise of discipline, or participation by a congregation may get out of hand. Many years ago I read an account of how early eighteenth-century Methodists lined hymns in the same way that many Blacks still do. The practice was suppressed among these Whites, however, because laity so often usurped the service, and "stole the show" with their virtuoso projections of the hymn lines. The day when that need returns to White mainline Protestantism is no doubt in the dim distance, if indeed it ever could return. But for those who fear the process of spontaneity, let the record show that every culture that ever practiced spontaneity in its rites has had a summary cure for those who departed from the purposes set forth in the cultural expectational script.

A PLAN FOR RECOVERY

For clergy and laity interested in implementing a return to dialogue in major brand worship, some suggestions are in order. The first has to do with the integrity of dialogue itself. No person seriously committed to it would dare breach the process by *sneaking* it into practice in public worship. However right one may know spontaneous response to be, the decision to use it cannot be made arbitrarily. *The decision to dialogue must be made in, yes, dialogue.*

Recent experiences with cultural concerns in Black middle-class churches have made me aware of just how sensitive such a subject can be. While many showed a fair degree of openness to freer congregational participation in the preaching experience, the same people were unbelievably rigid in their opposition to the "unholy inroads" of rhythm and fleshly gospel music, especially in their youth choirs. The reasons were always stated in ethical or theological terms, rather than culturally relative and discretionary language. However, the lie was given to this description when no opponent of drums in the Black churches concerned dared question the correctness of drums in a Pentecostal church context. The implication was clear; "religious jazz" was all right for that *class* of people. The breaking of association with class is difficult, but to bypass dealings with this deep conditioning only breeds opposition and contempt. Responsibility for the common culture must be exercised also in common and not unilaterally.

This holds true even when people are very open and permissive, letting the pastor of a dying church "try *anything.*" Culture is the transgenerational accumulation of the experience and insight of a given people. However irrational it may seem at present, it was probably formed on a very rational basis. The problem is that the cultural habit becomes ingrained and dissociated from the earlier functional basis. Like the inverted African pot for collecting sound and rendering clandestine slave worship undetectably silent, or like the Latin which Catholics held dear for so long, many of today's habits survive without a shred of basis. But they cannot be changed as quickly as pushing buttons on a computer. If people actively desire change, they still have to give their own depths reason, experiential exposure, and time to reorient or reprogram themselves.

The folk masses and the less-structured worship which I have encountered all over the country are so sterile because they have no authentic roots in previous culture. Things done on a drawing board cannot speak to the depths of personhood in worship, unless they take seriously and plug into what is already there. Dialogue as rootless fad and gimmick is worse than no dialogue at all. People must think and feel their way into it naturally.

Feeling one's way requires purposeful alterations in typical experiences and creative recombinations of familiar items. For instance, laity talk back to preachers all the time in one-on-one conversations and in small groups. It takes very little to expand on this, once reasoned understandings about direction have been arrived at. Small group meetings may be the scene of the introduction of dialogue, finally, into worship. People can comfortably try it on for fit, and the tapes can begin to collect in the depths. Not all who agree may be uninhibited enough to participate actively at first, or even at all, but, like all Black churches, they need only to affirm the practice and to enjoy its fulfillment vicariously. Little by little, freedom in the altered patterns will grow without destroying the worshipful mood or the rapport between worship leader and worshiper. The goal is irrepressible response, not well-trained claques.

The size of the group involved may be increased, but the starters must be a cadre of understanding and committed folk. Also, nonverbal dialogue should be greatly emphasized at first, with audible response introduced only when it can't be held back. It is well to remember that even in the Black model examined, only a minority actually respond audibly with any regularity. Sincerity is far more important than numbers in the matter of audible response.

As the process spreads and accelerates, exposures to cultural and/or denominational groups which have more audible dialogue may be helpful. But care must be taken to avoid either culture shock or culture-copying, and surface conformity to the "in" fad.

Finally, and above all, dialogue must be approached under

divine direction. No amount of careful planning and phasing can guarantee recovery. All one can do is plant and water, knowing that *God* gives the increase. If God does grant that audible dialogue may occur, it will. If he does not, and the group's openness is sincere, that in itself will immeasurably enrich worship, and the cross-fertilization of cultures will have achieved spiritual gains nevertheless.

8. Toward the Recovery of Preaching

WHAT HAS just been offered as a stratagem for the recovery of preaching dialogue must now be matched concerning the recovery of preaching as a whole. Whether recovery is thought of as the regaining of strengths long lost, or whether one denies the existence of viable cultural antecedents, the term recovery does apply to the need for new health in the vast majority of pulpits in America, in *all* cultures. To assume that this work can offer all the practical know-how would be sheer folly, but to refuse to attempt some concrete applications would be a cowardly stopping short of the very purpose for which the work was undertaken in the first place. Answers will be attempted in three areas: the dynamics of preaching—the roles assigned preachers and hearers; the theological assumptions undergirding these role assignments and the whole preaching task; and the goals and criteria for preaching, with this latter topic requiring the vast majority of this chapter.

THE ROLES IN PREACHING

The genius of the Black preaching model starts with the role assignments of the Black mass audience—the expectations, at least partially self-fulfilling, of the hearer hungry for a word of encouragement, nourishment, affirmation, and direction. Such expectations place on the preacher a burden which is both blessed and barely bearable. He is held in the esteem of an intimate father-figure, but serving at the same time as messenger from heaven and advocate of the members' just causes on earth. The Black preacher dares not take seriously or personally the high status accorded, but he dare not shrink from the role assignments, demanding though they may be. For the most part they are inseparable from the preaching. The consideration of dialogue has already established that homiletics is not an isolated art, and whatever the best of Black tradition may say to the generality of preachers must be understood, finally, in the larger context of the total task, although the focus in this work is on preaching.

In other words, the best of Black preaching, the kind that feeds and lifts and heals and moves persons, occurs in the warm context of a dynamic and mutually supportive ministry. The intimate rapport between pastor and parishioner is achieved by more than speaking charisma, and the openness and expectation of the hearer become a kind of conditioned response, applicable eventually to all or most of the preachers one hears. At the very least ordained ministers generally are assumed to have spiritual good to give unless and until their presentations prove the assumption utterly false.

This generous working hypothesis concerning preachers stems from the fact that Black preacher/pastors are literal father-figures of their congregations, which, as had been noted, are essentially extended families. Veneration for the elderly and long tenure, on boards as well as in the pulpit (thirty and even forty years are not uncommon), are all by-products of the basically African kinship character of the congregation/tribe— the brothers and sisters in Christ and in the oppressed community. This means that the title "Father," though seldom used in the less liturgical majority of Black churches, is literally descriptive of actual practice, perhaps more than in any other part of the Christian church. This has great bearing on the establishment of relations between preacher and hearer/responder. Unlike the professional and often adversary role assigned many White preachers, the Black pastor's role is that of welcome guide and needed resource. The gospel proclaimed is neither argument in debate nor any other external or abstract wisdom. It is the word of the family father who walks close with God and then conveys the eagerly awaited word he has received.

There was a time when the wider applicability or usefulness of such Black-culture insights were appraised very low. Precious little Black-to-White dialogue occurred between cultures because, no matter how good one's gifts, they had to be accepted as such to be useful. Whites weren't accepting then, for reasons already set forth. But, along with this greater openness, the climate of White understanding of their own needs is changing. Projections concerning America's ever more mobile, alienated and lonely society indicate that our only hope of remaining in a humanizing community relationship lies in a widespread, on-the-spot capacity to evolve "families" without blood ties—the kind that only idealistic groups like churches can develop. So the family climate so necessary to good Black-preaching rapport is essential to more than Blacks. An excellent model of the effectiveness of the extended family process is the manner in which the Black-Church/extended family served as an antidote for the earlier dehumanization potential of slavery, a dehumanization not altogether unlike that of modern White megalopolis. Just as slaves maintained African-style, stable and meaningful relations, calling everybody "Uncle" or "Aunt" or "Grandma," Blacks of the urban ghetto have used the same family instincts to survive.[1] And Hispanics and other ethnics, as well as some strata of Whites, have also formed families for psychic and physical survival. There are, thus, more than preaching reasons why the White middle-class church needs to acculturate back or forward to a Black/"primitive" *family*-church model.

A THEOLOGY OF PREACHING

That congregational kinship-type roles (the family of one God and Father) should be so important and so functional in the preaching event is illustrative of the functional significance of all sound Christian theology. However, the high esteem in which Blacks hold preaching comes not only from this cultural-theological kinship model and rapport, but also from folk belief about the way God himself ordains and uses preachers and preaching. The theological language refers to it as a divine vocation or call to preach. Whatever the inadequacies of the preacher-father, he has been given the benefit of the doubt and assumed anointed and worthy of the restraint exercised by David in reference to Saul: "Touch not mine anointed, and do my prophets no harm" (1 Chron. 16:22). Positively speaking the preacher has been *safe* to declare God's counsel. That he was called, like Jeremiah, while still waiting to be born (Jeremiah 1:5) is presumed true until proven otherwise. Black folk wait in awe for the fire shut up in the preacher's bones to be unleashed (Jer. 20:9), for they know that woe is he if he preach not the gospel (1 Cor. 9:16). Needless to say, the source material assumed for all this preaching is the Bible, although the Bible only confirmed a previous and profound African understanding of divine call.

This biblically based configuration of respect gives the Black preacher freedom to declare what he holds to be the will of God, regardless. And so long as the proclamation manifests sincerity and makes minimal sense, it would hardly occur to a Black congregation to challenge the propriety of the process or the preacher's right to freedom of speech in the pulpit. Such a climate of acceptance may beget laziness on part of some preachers, but for the most part it frees and empowers, encouraging creative, effective preaching. Dialogue may be more restrained while hearers weigh out a fresh insight or a prophetic challenge to one of their pet sins. But there are few if any vested interests to be protected, and personal habits are known to be fair game for any gospel sharpshooter. Preaching can never recover or flourish unless preachers are as courageous as Jeremiah, to be sure. But their word will be worthless unless they are confirmed in their pulpits by congregations who respect the preacher's right and obligation to say it to them.

The White church which laments a pop-gun caliber of preaching must accept the responsibility for having intimidated and dwarfed its prophets, as a matter of all too common tradition.

This negative movement has not been without help from White theologians, too, for they have moved against the divine call or vocation of preachers. In a misguided effort to equalize laity and remove arbitrary distinctions from among church persons, the professors and scholars have demoted both call and preaching, instead of elevating the sense of divine guidance in the laity's own lives.

Then White preachers themselves have had a part, failing even to see the need for divine involvement in a call to so narrow a role assignment. This view is quite unlike that of Black preachers, who contemplate with fear and trembling their taxing task of being so many things to so many needy people, and who, ideally, would not dare it save for a *supernatural summons.*

In the recovery of preaching there has to be a recovery of crucial gut feelings as well as theological understandings on the subject. The difference may be styled as that between a preacher-professional speaking almost unwillingly to an audience-employer with low expectations, on the one hand, and a divinely directed vessel of clay declaring the literal good news of the gospel, with power, on the other. I am continually amazed at the number of White seminary students who have real misgivings about preaching, or just hope not to have to do it. I was judgmental of them until it occurred to me that I wouldn't have aspired to preaching either, had I grown up with the image and understanding of preaching to which they were accustomed. The overhaul of the theology of preaching has to be drastic, with the burden borne by every facet of the White church. Denominational structures, clergy, and laity will have to shoulder the responsibility for hammering out a set of contemporary convictions concerning ministry which resurrect expectations and fire the preaching event with new creativity and courage, inspiration and impact.

GOALS AND CRITERIA

It is time now to practice what has been preached here, and to take the risk of declaring the counsel of God on the mechanics of the recovery of preaching, as I have seen that counsel expressed in Black tradition. It is risky because it is hard to think of much of it as really new, as it appears in print. Hopefully readers will couple the reading of this work with a new interest in getting *experiences* of the best of Black preaching, the distinctiveness and power of which are not capable of capture in paper and print. The "chemistry" of the elements and the proper proportions of each will come clearer in *experience* of the gift of the Black church. That gift, as portrayed here, has been described and analyzed by in-service classes of Black pastors, whose own list of criteria follows, setting forth the ideas they use to evaluate their own preaching and that of their peers.

The Primacy of Need

Preaching must speak to the human condition. However clever an idea, if it does not speak to real need it is useless. Preaching which authentically speaks to the need of one person speaks to the needs of that person's "race." Ultimately this means the *human* race. Mention has been made of the shocking failure of preachers to address the very needs they themselves feel, but the omission was not intentional. The problem arose from a failure to assess material in a disciplined way, with the result that preaching impact was squandered in the meeting of needs the preacher had as preacher rather than as person. The need to impress and have high impact must be subordinate to the need to feed—to give help to all those who are trapped in the human predicament.

 Every sermon introduction should focus on a sensitive living issue and claim, therewith, the undivided attention of the hearer, purely on the grounds of crying need. The only difference between the Black ghetto churches and the White churches in affluent suburbia is the visibility and nature of the needs. Both have great needs among every congregation. I knew of a White preacher whose facing and handling of the drug-abuse problems in his super comfortable community not only drew attendance and attention to his preaching; it saved his call to that church when the pressures generated by his Christian stand on housing discrimination threatened to evict him outright from the pulpit. Attention and acceptance are no problem when real needs are addressed.

People may, in some cultures, place a higher premium on a surface success image, but their spiritual needs and deep insecurities are as great as those of any other culture. And the preacher who speaks to those real needs commands their attention and ultimately their supportive response and loyalty.

The Authoritative Source

The Black religious tradition is not unique in viewing the Bible as the only source from which one would dare to speak. Needy Black audiences did not invent the practice of accepting answers only from the sole oracle recognized among them. Among all cultures the preacher must render it in his own very personal style, but the answer must be unmistakably rooted in the Word. However, in the Black model, this is not to be understood as a rigid literalism—bibliolatry and immature preoccupation with print. As has been stated here, just as the Bible books themselves were orally transmitted long before they were written down, so does the Black psyche still depend on the Bible as a cultural-religious heritage, based on the intimate and normative authority which grows out of the fact that one's parents and ancestors held it dear. They quoted it effectively and illustrated it with their lives. It has always been the authority of oral tradition that personal ancestors walked with God and interpreted that walk for their descendants. When captured Africans were brought to forced labor in the USA, the multilingual and multimythic host adapted to and adopted a new oral religious tradition (the Bible) in which all could take part together, since it was the tradition which prevailed on their new turf. Now, three hundred years later, that Canon of Scriptures is the accepted "tradition of the Blackamerican ancestors." *Literal* inspiration of the Bible, as defined in some

White disputes, is not in the least at issue. "My grandmother told me . . . " is far more binding for a verse at gut level, and that is the authority Black preaching comes from.

Because the method of transmittal of the tradition is alive, the oral tradition itself and its interpretation are also alive and dynamic. Words and their standard definitions are important, but the spirit of address is more important than the letter of the interpretation. So persons relate to the gospel as shared *experience,* as well as shared idea and literature. The Word is not aloof, since it is part of a heritage *personally* possessed in an extended family. And the preacher's deep personal involvement in his/ her heritage also is contagious.

There is perhaps no greater contribution which Black religion could make to the churches of the Euro-American majority than this: a release from dispute over the Bible. On the one hand are the hide-bound literalists, investing unbearable significance in commas and periods, and on the other are the modern minded, whose scientific understandings are well documented, but whose relation to the power and authority of the Word leaves something to be desired. The Black tradition meets the demands of both, while *escalating* the overall high esteem and everyday interest in which the Bible is held as Word of God. There is no race, culture, or theological persuasion which would not respond to a lively, Black-type repertoire of interesting characters and meaningful stories from Scripture. This could go a long way towards the recovery of preaching everywhere. There is power in the contagion of a serious believer whose message is dynamic and human and contemporary, but dominated totally by a living biblical tradition.

The Focus on a Clearly Defined Goal

Of course, the sermon text assumed in the foregoing treatment must be chosen by the final guidance of God, who has called the preacher in the first place; but that choice must be made in conjunction with the choice of a goal or purpose for the sermon. This seems simple and obvious enough, but it has turned out to be the single most difficult aspect of the introductory preaching course among practicing pastors, as well as among students of various cultures. The problems lie in the fact that the rhetoric about preaching and the subtle personal satisfactions in preaching do not match the realities and requirements of transconscious impact. Almost invariably the preacher/student will say that "The goal is to *show* . . ." The announced purpose will be clearly and exclusively to enlighten—"a head trip," as we say. Chapter 3 has set forth the need to speak to *all* sectors of human consciousness. And this simply must be reflected in the goal.

"To show" has such a strong and subtle hold on preachers because it appeals to vanity, providing opportunity to share one's clever interpretations or startling distinctions between things. But even to seek with all humility to "show" a major doctrine is a goal shorn of the full intent of the gospel. The irony of it all, in spite of the limitations of the typically stated objectives, is that Black preachers have historically set out to *move* persons, even if they did nothing else. Yet students will announce in class and on the outline a totally intellectual purpose. It is time for all of us honestly to embrace the goal of a *complete* gospel, which includes the deep *moving* of persons, perhaps above all else, and sets forth an abstract rationale as well. Well-meant bows to academia and poorly disguised attempts "to show" great ideas, and thus "show off," must alike give way to the purpose of a new *total* person in Christ.

The movement of persons is not just limited to what is referred to as emotion. There is also movement from one level of growth and spiritual maturity to another, from one level of commitment to another, and from one pattern of concrete action to another more like unto Christ. When the classes mentioned had wrestled through to a commitment to reaching the *total person transconsciously*, goals shifted to heavier emphasis on things like changed value systems and tables of priority, changed objects of trust, and changed aspects of interpersonal relations. It was agreed, eventually, that no doctrine about God, even, is only to be "shown" and believed intellectually. Each belief has a counterpart or reflection in human life. When Jesus spoke of the forgiveness of God, he always had a human goal more than simply "showing." The Parable of the Forgiving Father or Prodigal Son was to raise trust levels so that persons would arise and go to their forgiving Father (Luke 15). The Parable of the Unmerciful Servant (Matt. 18:21–35) spoke also of how God's forgiveness must be reflected in the forgiveness of persons. *Every* great religious idea has a performance response, demanding a more comprehensive and realistic preaching goal, and providing a surprisingly solid and helpful discipline in the preparation of a sermon.

Class after class has conceded that when the text and goal have been properly clarified and "fine-tuned," understood and related, the sermon is half finished. Or, at very least, its direction and momentum have been so well established as to make the rest relatively easy. Decisions about the relevance or usefulness of any given item, idea or illustration are easy to make. And so are the other decisions, about time limits, redundancy, timing or pace, and climax. What once may have seemed like ruthless rejection of good material in the interest of time turns out to be the disciplined delay of the employment of a "goody" until one is called to preach towards a goal which it might better serve. One only needs the faith to believe that there will be another time to preach, and that one's pride will not suffer unduly from the postponement of the flashy use of one particular pearl of wisdom. Knowing there will be other sermons and even better pearls, the preacher hues to the goal at hand with easy discipline and better focus and flow.

It is not that great ideas have no value, but simply that the idea must have a living application as its end. Ideas were made to lift up people, and not people to lift up ideas. Studying pastors hardly ever actually practiced an idea-glorifying pulpit ministry, but when "to show" was ruled out of written outlines, they yielded with difficulty. They brought in goals like "to help the saints realize that . . . " and "to reaffirm the value . . . " Even when the person-oriented goals were accepted, there were abstract expressions of purpose like "to inspire individual and corporate participation in the celebration of life." There is a subtle but tremendous difference in the rewrite of purpose for the "saints" mentioned above: "to help storm-tossed saints trust their anchor in Christ." Whereas the goal "to help the saints realize that" was focused on a *fact* immediately following, the new goal addressed both the logical doubts and battered feelings which prevent trust, and allowed for an experience of celebration in which trustful feelings were expanded. This does not destroy the original purpose, it fulfills it.

The rewards of staying with a text and goal are astounding. The stereotypical wanderings of many preachers have confused some of the very elect, so that the gratitude which students report given for clarity almost exceeds reason at times. Most people have come to expect that there will be much which they cannot understand. Or, if they can understand the parts, they will find it next to impossible to fit them into a coherent whole. When they can't see the thread of meaning or theme which runs from text and introduction through to the climax, the presentation amounts to a mishmash of ideas to them—an uncertain blast on the trumpet. Laity are greatly disconcerted by the question, "Just what am I supposed to *do* as a result of this message?" Persons from 8 to 108 want guidance, and they are eternally grateful when it is plainly and relevantly given.

Preaching is teaching; a sermon destitute of ideas is poor fare indeed. But the goal must be to plant the ideas in the *totality* of human consciousness, which begets matching behavior as well as belief. Jesus judged the latter by the former—the fruit.

The Point as Positive

In addition to the traditional Black commitment to move persons there is another powerful intuition which is almost never articulated, except by sage old preachers: the commitment to affirmation. The old Fathers of the Black pulpit said it in terms of catching more flies with honey than with vinegar, and Henry Sloan Coffin[2] warned Union Seminary classes against using the pulpit for a whipping post. Somehow unaware of this, the pastor-student rushes to class with his jewel, only to be reminded that the agreed upon criterion against negative impact rules out most of the sermon's appeal. There and then the process of revision is begun, seeking to flesh out the positive side of the same idea, to a *two-thirds majority of the sermon*. The preacher is not always willing, especially when it turns out that some of the cleverest negatives have very little positive counterpart. The argument is often advanced that there are times when congregations *need* to be spanked, and when they know it themselves and welcome it. This is reflected in the masochistic but commonplace reality that it is often easier to stir response with spectacular criticism than with great affirmation. The fact is more likely and relevant that it is easier to *prepare* for bombardment than for building. The gospel is and must ultimately remain *good* news, and the easily stirred responsiveness of people who have already been taught to hate themselves is the last thing a preacher ought to want to appeal to. In fact, the psychiatric profession is so very leary of most religion largely because so much of it is unnecessarily guilt producing, and damaging to healthy self-acceptance and maturity. The recovery of preaching has to involve the recovery of the positive.

I have already contrasted the fiery utterance of the White mass-media pulpit with the Black pulpit thus: "fiery mad" as opposed to "fiery glad." It is obviously an oversimplification, and my own class members don't measure up to it at times. But it has enough truth to demand attention. The celebration which takes place in the best of Black sermon climax has always been on positive themes like the goodness of God, or "Ain't He all right!"; "Bread in a starving land;" and "He's my doctor." So widely characteristic of Black folk-preaching tradition, these themes are unmistakably affirmation. To be sure, the latter is often engaged in after the main body of a message rather completely unrelated—a climax tacked on for effect. However, the integrity of preaching demands at *all* times a harmony and identity between the celebration at the end and the preceding material. Goals of transconscious change also require the focus of the total message on the positive point. The recovery of preaching simply depends heavily on religious affirmation in a shaky society, and the prophet who would criticize that society and cry for justice can achieve his or her holy ends better by positively declaring God's justice than by belaboring unjust fellow citizens overmuch.

The Native Tongue of the Hearer

The chief motivation for the study of Black preaching by classes of pastors already well along in preaching experience may be summed up in the following quotation from the criteria they jointly adopted:

> Speak in the Black idiom and cultural frame of reference for a significant portion of the time, identifying with and communicating with the Black masses, and yet establishing a model of bi-cultural fluency and wider concern.

The class members want to stay close to their constituencies, and they welcome a training program committed to keeping rather than destroying the speech signals that bind them to their people.

Yet the foregoing chapter on "Preaching as Folk Language," is resisted by many Black professionals (preachers included), as evidenced in my first exploration of the subject which appeared in *Black Preaching* in 1970. What is behind this formal resistance to something most Black preachers actually practice so completely—this hue and cry against Black English? One answer already mentioned is simply that people wish to use language for something besides communication, namely personal image projecting and status-seeking. Before one can finish explaining the total objective by mention of the bicultural fluency so widely needed, the hypersensitive opponent is off on a harangue. However, my own experience mentioned early in chapter 6 is evidence enough that the exclusive use of "standard" English, the dialect of middle-class mid-America, can actually impede the hearing of the gospel in the Black ghetto. People respond best to *some* hearing of their native tongue, whether they be "mountain people" from Appalachia, Mexican Americans, or anybody else. The best compliment you can pay them is to join them in their speech, as evidenced by the huge and growing popularity of "country and western" music. To the extent that the accurate hearing of religious profundities and nuances is dependent upon the use of the mother tongue of the hearer, there can be no argument, finally, against the use in preaching of some form of Black English or other nonstandard or indigenous group speech. Preachers need also to use fluency in every possible experiential and linguistic frame of reference common to those with whom they have to communicate.

As previously stated, this is not to promote an "Amos-and-Andy" dialect, but it is to rule out the equally extreme and utterly foreign exclusive dependence on clipped, cold, and very "correct" media English. Positively stated, that is to say that if one already naturally sounds like a Martin Luther King or a Jesse Jackson, that person penetrates and is more acceptable just because deep understanding for the Black world is made easier. Whole, subtle worlds of meaning that would otherwise be lost can be conveyed by what Blacks sometimes call a "home" pattern of speech. So much is wrapped up in language that to fight native speech is to erode identity itself, as well as to sacrifice significance. Less is said of regional and class speech groups, but the appeal of nonstandard English in an important percentage of religious radio and television may suggest greater warmth and deeper religious emotion in the regions and classes whose speech is much closer to Oral Roberts than to John Chancellor.

The implications in the wider world are no less sweeping. A substantial proportion of the vocational problems and frustrations which are driving so many young White clerics to drop out of ministry of pastorates can literally be traced to cultural impasse, brought on by training in a seminary establishment which wars against the religious patterns of ordinary Whites (cf. chapter 2). Most credentialed pastors arrive at their first parishes having been for three or four years acculturated away from the vocabulary and mental images, the frame of reference and basic concerns of that portion of the population which seminaries and others have pilloried as the "silent majority." Whatever their limits, and no Black person can forget their demonic prejudices, they have a human birthright to be taught in their own tongue. If that requires that their M.Div. minister sound strangely similar to a nineteenth-century revivalist or, in other words, overly "conservative," that is the risk that has to be taken to lead the sheep out of the darkness into the marvelous light.

Dialects are only a highly visible or audible and concrete minority of the total cultural issue. When one "sits where they sit," respecting their integrity as persons, sensing the reality of their predicament and the fact that they too have ideals, one easily and naturally identifies with the flock. If and when this takes place, the matter of tongue will solve itself, unconsciously, with the preacher subtly accommodating language to *avoid contrast* with significant persons in his or her world. This is not a compromise; it is simply an adjustment in communications to empower the preacher to lead the congregation to pastures of greater spiritual maturity *and* social justice.

Communication with the Whole Person

The challenge to choose and use a significant portion of the speech nearest the native tongue of the hearer stems from more than the undeniable need for linguistic identity and bond between speaker and hearer. It stems from more, also, than Black youth's need for a bicultural model of fluency in a society dominated by another culture. The chief basis for the linguistic challenge above is the *profound influence of idiom on communication with the whole person.* The language closest home conveys the subtle and intimate nuances of meaning, using "frequencies" beyond the common tongue of marketplace and intercultural small talk.

Again, a goal approved by several classes of Black pastors is highly significant and instructive:

Seek to communicate with all sectors of human consciousness, not just the rational. Include the intuitive and the still more deeply repressed wounds, wisdom and wonder of Black existence, those aspects of personhood too often lightly dismissed as "emotional." Communicate sincerely from personal depths.

A great deal is required in addition to the broad-channel language capabilities just dealt with, if one is to reach the goal of communication with all sectors of human consciousness, however.

So grand an enterprise must necessarily emanate from all sectors of the speaker's consciousness. Deep must call unto deep—personal depth speaking to personal depth. The speaker who has no deep feelings and convictions, therefore, is without anything to say. Nevertheless, there is far more profound belief hidden in the depths of most functioning persons than the Euro-American cultural ethos usually permits to surface. The overcoming of the bias against the very certainties by which persons literally bet their whole lives is the first step toward recovery of preaching to the whole person. The speaker has to recover the content of the transconscious depths that are to call out to the deep consciousness of others. There are a variety of ways to sift for one's real convictions, whatever the specific race or culture involved. I have often assumed a devil's advocate role and argued fiercely with a student who supposedly had nothing in his depths about which to speak or write. A tape, of course, was recording, and the gut response soon came out, often eloquently. The task, thereafter, was simply one of editing a flow which came in a passionate burst of freedom from culturally and/or academically imposed spiritual inhibition.

Another version of the above tactic was employed many years ago to help a prospective pastor too timid to verbalize direct resistance to a formidable inquisitor. He wrote his supposedly meager meanings in briefs, as a response to written prodding. In the process he lost some of his far-out and surplus intellectual baggage, but far more importantly, he recovered consciousness of a tremendous wellspring of positive world view or folk-conviction. He recovered beliefs of which he had lost consciousness through a lifetime spent in academic circles. He had *lived* by these convictions, and he soon sensed the need to proclaim them to persons who had not had his rich Christian upbringing, or whose faith, like his, needed update and cultivation.

Still another approach in this same vein has worked well with that vast majority of persons who had only a few really deep convictions of which they were rationally conscious. Charged by the instructor to preach only from that small belief base, they have watched it expand rapidly as the logical relatedness of this faith to other hidden faith has emerged.

It is also true that the congregation's folk-response to deep conviction concerning foundational tenets of faith has contributed to this heightened awareness of what has been hidden. Faith, once shelved in response to fancied peer pressure in an unreal academic atmosphere, bursts forth in new power when encouraged by a new set of significant persons in one's life—a congregation of folk whose evident hungers and needs are both inspirational and instructive.

Several professionally trained Blacks have been moved from the status of learned pulpit supply to beloved official pastor simply because they learned so quickly to respond to the congregation's cry, as well as to articulate depths of personal faith temporarily hidden. I think especially of one Black theological professor whose recovery was quicker than the pulpit committee's search for a "real" preacher, so that he was soon asked to serve one of America's great Black congregations.[3] Twelve years later he resigned teaching even part-time to conduct one of the most remarkable preaching and community-oriented ministries in the church today.[4] His old and nourishing instincts and intuitions were coaxed out of hiding by the logical expansion of a belief base never destroyed, and by his creative dialogue with a great congregation, as well as with his wise old preacher father. His name is William Holmes Borders, pastor of the Wheat Street Baptist Church of Atlanta.

The whole person who communicates intelligently with the whole of the consciousness of other persons is all too rare, because of a fantastically pervasive misreading of how whole persons hear. I have recently encountered American-influenced curriculum at an African Seminary, purporting to teach preachers to construct arguments and devise points after the manner of American Whites. How tragic! How wasteful of an indigenous culture which has communicated effectively with the human transconscious for literally centuries, in folk narrative.

Not only is deep conviction repressed by Euro-American culture; the preached message is almost exclusively beamed to that aspect of personhood least capable of all-out belief—the rational conscious. In other words, if trained preachers Black and White have succeeded in reaching and touching more than conscious reason, it has been in spite of the Western intellectual frame of reference and not because of it.

Black preaching tradition is the grandparent of the "soul" so widely associated with Black music. And one of the tradition's greatest possible gifts to the church at large is a model of soul communication-preaching that speaks to *all* the sectors of consciousness, summed up in the term *soul*. What does this require?

In addition to deep convictions which cry for expression, this soul signal system requires freedom to express feeling in natural ways such as body movement and language vehicles which facilitate the process. The subtleties of word and phrase and how they impact on the soul are especially important. For instance, declarative sentences, or fact, may establish an iron-clad case for an ideal or an ethical principle. Unless the facts are unusually startling, the realm of impact will be limited to the rational conscious. Since so much of behavior emanates from other sectors, the goal of moving whole souls or persons will be lost. A signal with wider impact than declarative sentences is required.

Pictures and poetry, narratives of human struggle, and descriptions of deep feeling all have that wider impact on the soul. Beauty penetrates and stirs up action where logic only begets empty assent; yet lasting beauty must be an expression and extension of the greatest truths. It is a matter of a Martin

Luther King, Jr., choosing to share a vision of constitutional democracy, a dream, rather than giving a logical Gettysburg Address, the immortal importance of which dawned on the world *after* its delivery. Yet even Lincoln's great speech had a beauty—a tightly packed elegance which, with the years of familiarity, has given it impact not attained on first hearing.

It has been said that a picture is worth a thousand words, but it is also true that a word picture skillfully and sensitively drawn may have the impact of a thousand sound arguments. I think, for instance, of a former college president, incidentally White, who indelibly etched the prelude to the crucifixion on my memory. His picture included well-researched details about the hobnailed boots of a Roman soldier, appealing insights into the soldier's human reaction to the Jews' universal disdain for his noisy boots and untenable authority, and the spiritual stature of Jesus, quietly being torn by whip thongs with metal tied in at intervals. No camper at that hilltop vesper service will be the same after that. Learned and moving pictures like that need to replace a great deal of the arguments and artless declaration of today's pulpit.

The best of the Black preaching tradition abounds in pictures and poetic phrase, but it is at its best in narratives—folk tales and epic encounter of the spirit, as found in the Bible and to a lesser extent in the lives of ordinary contemporaries. This phase of the Black tradition's gift justifies separate treatment; it is the ultimate example of communicating with the whole person.

The Story as Total Communication

The Black pulpit is at its best when the gospel is communicated in the form of a folk story. That is to say, there is no better vehicle for the unforgettable portrayal of a powerful truth than an engaging tale; and the Black tradition has excelled in this art form. After all the issues were faced and adequate freedom from Western models of communication was achieved, my classes have agreed with me that no other form should be used in preference to a good story. When one uses an intellectual argument or essay form, it ought to be either an adjunct to a shorter story or a choice growing out of the fact that one has no story suitable for that particular gospel idea. It is no accident that Black preachers ask of another preacher, "Can he tell the story?"

Chapter 3 on "Preaching as Meaningful Experience" has set forth the rationale for this stand in greater detail. The purpose here is simply to summarize and sharpen the narrative goal and priority in the context of the summary of all the goals.

A first and foremost objective in the taletelling generating of meaningful experience is that of an "eyewitness account." This sums up the manner of one whose experience has been so real as to be capable of contagious sharing. In a word, it means that the teller has lived with the biblical account so long as to have seen it almost literally. The minutest details which contribute to the atmosphere and ultimate understanding are shared with the ease and enthusiasm of one present when it happened. Those who hear are thus contagiously caught up in the same meaningful experience, being both delighted and enlightened.

What appears to be a casual delivery, however, requires no less discipline than did the tales of the African-culture precursors of the Black pulpit story. In fact, the type of details once easily memorized from traditional tellers in Africa and elsewhere have now to be dug out by serious study for the contemporary pulpit of all cultures. Hours of early research for all available hard data in the literature of biblical scholarship are followed by later hours of meditation and mental association. The preacher-teller has to weave it all together by inspired and enlightened imagination, so that the picture during preaching emerges clear, and the characters to be portrayed or acted come through familiar and real. Like the earlier African audiences, the contemporary Christian audience knows when the imaginative details stray wide of the Bible truth and goal. And yet their very attentiveness is a form of demand that their understandings be stretched and their souls moved by a combination of fresh insight and original style along with the old, old story.

As the classes have come to agree, this kind of preaching requires five or six days of the week just to live one's way into the story and its acting parts. Thus, while the outline of a one-story sermon may seem easy, the process of research and breathing breath into the bones of hard data is much more demanding. Special care has to be taken with details so as to give enough, but to avoid misleading surplus. It all depends on the point; a given tale may be told a dozen ways, with as many different sets of details and as many different goals. Such has been the case as classes have dealt with "The Prodigal Son." However, the fact that one has not the homework and imagination to tell even one good story may be reason enough to settle for the less effective essay style.

There are, nevertheless, some consoling alternatives for the young and less imaginative preacher, unable to find a good sermon story to tell so seldom as once a quarter. One such alternative is that a very good gospel goal may be advanced by a declarative rather than a narrative text, which may be illustrated by many shorter and therefore easier stories. These may also be instructive and memorable. Another consolation is that one stores and *accumulates* pithy details for really good folk narratives and characters as one gains experience. After a few years one gets the "hang" of it and can work from an increasingly rich personal repertoire. Thirdly, there is a communal repertoire of tales and details that builds up through the years. It is not plagiarism to tell a story somewhat as previously heard, unless one puts no new insight or personal style into the rendition. Indeed, one of the purposes of this work is to encourage the expansion of a rapidly depleting communal or folk repertoire of gospel stories among Black preachers and whosoever else is willing. Thus the ideal of narrative creativity is made less of a burden, and the stories, known by laity and clergy alike, become a part of a dynamic context which increases both dialogue and effectiveness in preaching.

The point is simply that the assertions of reason alone are sorely limited as to both conceptual accuracy and impact on persons. Nothing important should ever be said by syllogism which is not also stated more comprehensively in symbolic story, poetry, or picture. The latter is better remembered as well as more moving of persons, while the former is only remembered when stated in clever and often simplistic aphorism. The gospel is bigger than that, requiring the broad-channel communication of artistic elements addressing the whole person.

The structure of the story-sermon, however, is not greatly different from the structure of all preaching, so that aspect is dealt with in the following section on flow and timing.

Structure and Pace

Several simple rules of composition must be observed if preaching is to benefit generally from the Black pulpit heritage. This is true both in and out of the Black church, since much of the natural intuitional genius that originally established these guidelines among them has been eroded, if indeed it ever was widespread:

1. Sequence the events or points-with-illustration in an order of ascending or increasing emotional impact. Hopefully this sequence will match some logical or chronological treatment, but the order of feeling takes precedence over all other orders, since descending emotional impact is anticlimactic and cancels attention.

This, of course, assumes and makes specific the serious concern to develop emotional impact, a cardinal assumption in Black preaching. Because it has been thought in most academic circles that acceptable emotion was utterly and unpredictably in the hands of the Holy Spirit, many modern Black preachers, like all the rest, have failed to weigh or predict impact. The result has been premature sermonic climax, followed either by a strained attempt to go still higher, or a terrible feeling that the sermon had gone flat and was inexorably petering out. Happy is the preacher who, having missed sensing the real climax during sermon preparation, senses conclusion when it actually happens, and deletes the balance of the sermon. In other words, when the Holy Spirit has deeply stirred a congregation climactically, it is not for the preacher to say that it was done in error or at the wrong place.

2. To ascending sequence must be added the smooth flow of good transition. Whatever the sermon type, the movement from incident to incident, scene to scene, or point to point must be signaled, and the junctions carefully planned. The first sentence of this paragraph is an obvious example of transition: the words that tell the hearer that we are moving now to the next stage.

The instructor may seem overly demanding at this point, but the student needs only to listen to the sermons of other preaching students to see how crucially important such transitional signals are. Even fellow preachers with outlines in hand often have a hard time following each other's ideas. Since hearers from the laity have no script and only one chance to make sense of it, the rules for sermon outlining are even more functional and unchangeable than the rules governing the outlining of theses. Many outlines, including those of the writer, may be quite condensed and topical, at every point save the *transitions*. There the wording is verbatim; it is that important. Sermons may have anywhere from two to four points between the introduction and the conclusion or climax, or the latter may also be the last point. Still another possibility may be that the whole sermon will be just one extended story, with meaningful asides. But whatever the structure (there is no uniquely Black sermon outline), and however good the narrative illustration, the thread of meaning must be easily ascertainable on first hearing because of carefully prepared *transition*.

3. Proper flow and timed impact lead to a special kind of climactic utterance. In chapter 4 on "Preaching as Celebration," sermonic climax has been dealt with and illustrated at length. The guidelines governing good climax are summarized here: (a) Great themes beget great

summary or climactic utterance. This is always affirmative or in the positive vein, declaring the news which is good. (b) Good climax includes real gratitude for needs met; in effect it is the celebration which attaches to the feasting of the soul. (c) Good climax includes heightened audience participation and the personal expression and fulfillment of the congregation. (d) Good climax also celebrates rather than introduces new insights, since these should have been presented and elaborated much earlier. (e) Thus climax grows out of the main body of the sermon, not just alongside it. Climax which does not grow from the main portion of the sermon is obviously manipulative. (f) Good climax is characterized by celebrative *feelings* related to the ideas of the sermon and stated in feeling, poetic language. (g) This means that whether the climax includes a personal testimony or some other climactic narrative the emphasis must be on genuine expression of positive *feeling,* in which the speaker is personally and sincerely involved. (h) Since no amount of the following of such guidelines as this can guarantee authentic climax, perhaps the most important thing one does is to trust God after having done one's best.

IN CONCLUSION

The Black preaching tradition past, present, and future deserves more analysis and reflection than I have given here, but, at the time time, I think I have given as much as I should try to give in one book. On a subject so dear, there is a need for discipline, so that one shares one's best rather than one's all.

There should be more books about Black preaching, but not too many more. The tradition is oral, and the chief means of learning about it ought still to be oral. No other means will ever do it justice. The printed word can never be more than a substitute for the spoken word in any culture, and especially in Black. The attempt to capture Black preaching completely in print is forever doomed to failure. The most it can do is raise issues and establish something akin to criteria—the sort of thing which, being not oral but subtly intuitive in many cases, might otherwise be lost.

There does need to be a great deal of writing, however. The scholarship and details that could expand one's repertoire of characters ought not have to start from zero in every Black preacher, or in any other preacher in the world. There need to be more books like Leslie Weatherhead's *Personalities of the Passion.* Those with the talent should burst forth with a stream of the best tradition of folk-story renditions of Bible scenes and persons much as Clarence Jordan has done. Those who don't feel comfortable doing this hard research can then "do their thing" in the *telling of the stories.* Too many preachers are now dependent on alien essay-type aids which destroy the very character and integrity of their preaching. The stories, of course, will still require a personal touch, but they will raise deeply human concerns and give the answers of the preacher's own understanding of the gospel.

Like the spirituals, a published repertoire of engaging and instructive folk/oral stories from the biblical tradition should be available to Black and White, laity and clergy. Somewhat as Joel Chandler Harris preserved African-rooted animal tales with deeper meaning and gave what was not his for the world's enlightenment and enjoyment, Black scholars/preachers and others must seriously work at preserving and updating the genius of the Black and/or Southern Bible raconteur. The not altogether unique gift of the Black pulpit would then be easy to share with everybody. It might even become as contagious and popular as another gift of the Black experience—the jazz and soul music which dominate entertainment all over the world. I pray that it may be so, and I suspect that if the gospel were to be that popular, the world would be greatly helped. It might even be saved.

9. Postscript

WHAT I have tried to say, in a nutshell, is that preaching is a creature of the people and not of the lecture halls and libraries of the great church bodies. The divorce of popular practice and folk culture from organized religion, to the extent that it exists, has occurred because the established churches moved out and away. It was not because rampant materialism and atheistic or agnostic intellectualism drove a wedge. Materialism and worship of affluence have long since been baptized and confirmed, and the intellectualism is even further from the folk than the churches are. The recovery of preaching will occur only when it comes back to the people.

Far from being an avant-guard experiment, it is actually a return to a "primitive" sophistication about how faith is shared, nourished, and refined. Transconscious communication is a matter of using the mouth-to-ear methods that planted folk faith in the first place. Thus beliefs and trusts once transmitted by stories, until they were part of the deepest consciousness (usually misleadingly referred to as the unconscious), must be resurrected, pruned and improved, or replaced to provide better tales for today. The good news of the highest revelation of the Hebrew-Christian tradition must be given folk accessibility surpassing all paperbacks, comic books, movies or even TV, although it might employ all of these media.

This is not, of course, to suggest that the pulpit become even more of a poll parrot of popular views. Rather, on issues, it must evolve into the fifth column of the Kingdom of God, indistinguishable from the natives only in the surface matters of provincial taste and imagery that necessarily govern communication of every sort. The increased capacity for conveying messages can then be devoted to a much more risky and even at times radical declaration/experience of the Word and Will of God for the freeing and abundant life of all his children.

This more provincial signal system is more powerful because it is more familiar to all sectors of consciousness, reaching more aspects of the real person. It has been referred to here as transconscious communication. It will be extremely demanding, especially until a folk repertoire of contemporary meaningful gospel tales has been established, but it is very rewarding, and it is long overdue in most American pulpits.

A recent conversation with an overseas minister (once called a missionary) and a local pastor in Central Africa helped me to see this as never before. We were pondering the problem of freeing persons from the fear of spells. It was plain that mere reason and scientific insight were powerless in most instances. Degrees as high as Ph.D. had not helped local African Christians to conquer the dread of curses, both intended and unintentional. The answer had to be transconscious access to the aspects of persons where superstitious world views were stored. A replacement was needed for the tales and related conversation that had shaped this awful and involuntary slavery to the witchcraft extremes of a once positive as well as powerful traditional religion/medicine. The Gospel was full of higher tales for the purpose, but nobody had sensed their potential, even though it was plain that they must have "told the story" with healing results many times. Conscious employment of the gospel in the powerful folk idiom was all that was needed to multiply the healing and liberating results.

Then the light turned on. I suddenly remembered how utterly but unconsciously Americans are also enslaved to unnamed fears hidden deep in the psyche, out of the reach of reason. My wife and I had almost laughed our way through a showing of *The Exorcist,* while a theater full of young and unbelieving geniuses from a great university nearby had squirmed and shuddered through the dredging up of all of the demons they thought they never had. College religious centers and local pastors were flooded with sudden interest in an orthodox antidote for the ancient world view still stored so successfully in their very bones. They were second to fifth generation products of families of a faith debilitated by weak gospel as much as by strong secularism. The "faith of *their* fathers" was, like the gospel that begat it, lodged only in the regions of reason. Feelings and the emotional excesses of "primitive" religion had long since been ruled out. So the middle class's inescapable heritage of Salem witchcraft and its counterparts had been swept under the rug—repressed, as they say, for many generations.

What I found myself prescribing for supposedly primitive African pastors turned out to be no less necessary for the most learned pastors in the United States. The human predicament is universal. What planted, yea burned, positive gospel into the hearts of American slaves and freed many of them from all significant vestiges of blind superstition will still work in their homeland of Africa and in America's affluent suburbs as well. It is nothing less than the whole Gospel transmitted to a whole person. It has been labeled here the genius of Black preaching, but it is obviously the subtle genius of *all* preaching that has ever freed anybody anywhere. And it is needed today, by whatever name, wherever the human predicament is still experienced.

Notes

2. PREACHING AS FOLK CULTURE

1. John S. Mbiti, *African Religions and Philosophy* (New York: Praeger, 1969), p. 275.
2. C. G. Jung, *Psychology and Religion* (New Haven: Yale University Press, 1938), pp. 1–39.
3. Mircea Eliade, *Patterns in Comparative Religion,* trans. Rosemary Sheed (New York: Sheed & Ward, 1958), p. 434.
4. Mac Linscott Ricketts, "The Nature and Extent of Eliade's Jungianism," *Union Seminary Quarterly Review* 25, no. 2 (Winter 1970):221.
5. Eliade, *Patterns,* pp. 429–31.
6. Ibid., pp. 454–55, and Ricketts, *"Nature,"* p. 221.
7. Thomas A. Harris, *I'm OK—You're OK* (New York: Harper & Row, 1967; New York: Avon Books, 1973, p. 62).
8. Fanita English, "TA: A Populist Movement," *Psychology Today* 6, 11 (April 1973):48.
9. Harris, *I'm OK—You're OK,* p. 66.
10. Miles Mark Fisher, *Negro Slave Songs in the United States* (New York: Russell & Russell, 1968), p. 33.
11. Bruce A. Rosenberg, *The Art of the American Folk Preacher* (New York: Oxford University Press, 1970), pp. 3–8.
12. William H. Pipes, *Say Amen, Brother!* (Westport, Conn.: Negro Universities Press, 1970), p. 60.
13. Vernon Loggins, *The Negro Author: His Development in America to 1900* (Port Washington, N.Y.: Kennikat Press, 1964), p. 4. Cf. E. Franklin Frazier, *The Negro Church in America* (New York: Schocken Books, 1963), pp. 8–9.
14. Pipes, *Say Amen, Brother!,* pp. 60–61.
15. Ibid.

16. Leslie H. Fishel, Jr., and Benjamin Quarles, *The Negro American: A Documentary History* (Glenview, Ill.: Scott, Foresman, 1967), p. 135. Cf. also Eugene Genovese, *Roll, Jordan Roll: The World the Slaves Made* (New York: Vintage Books, 1976), p. 267.

3. PREACHING AS MEANINGFUL PERSONAL EXPERIENCE

1. George P. Rawick, *The American Slave: A Composite Autobiography* (Westport, Conn.: Greenwood, 1972), vol. 3, part 4, pp. 178–179.

4. PREACHING AS CELEBRATION

1. Henry H. Mitchell, *Black Preaching* (New York: J. B. Lippincott, 1970), p. 189.

5. PREACHING AS BIBLICAL STORYTELLING

1. Benjamin E. Mays, *Born to Rebel* (New York: Scribner's, 1971), p. 36.
2. Howard Thurman, *Jesus and the Disinherited* (Nashville: Abingdon, 1949), pp. 30–31.
3. Maya Angelou, *I Know Why the Caged Bird Sings* (New York: Random House, 1969), pp. 18, 26, 31, 55–56, 96–100, 191.
4. Story-sermon by Henry H. Mitchell, August 6, 1951, at "Junior Citizens Camp." Pinecroft, Colfax, California.
5. Richard M. Dorson, *American Negro Folktales* (New York: Fawcett, 1967), p. 49.
6. Ibid.
7. Ibid., pp. 50–53.
8. Ibid., p. 52.
9. Sojourner Truth, *Narrative of Sojourner Truth* (Chicago: Johnson, 1970), p. 83.
10. Ibid., p. 130.
11. Clarence Jordan, "The Rich Man and Lazarus, and Other Parables Retold for Our Time," a sound recording released by Koinonia Records, Tiskilwa, Ill. 61368.

6. PREACHING AS FOLK LANGUAGE

1. William Labov, *The Social Stratification of English in New York City* (Washington, D.C.: Center for Applied Linguistics, 1966), p. 482.
2. "Booming, Bodacious Citizens Band Radio," *Reader's Digest* 109, 652 (August 1976): 72–74, condensed from *Time,* 10 May 1976.
3. Labov, *Social Stratification,* p. 475.
4. Ibid., pp. 410 ff.

5. John Lovell, Jr., *Black Song: the Flame and the Forge* (New York: Macmillan, 1972), p. 307.
6. A close parallel to this may be found in Harold A. Carter's *The Prayer Tradition of Black People* (Valley Forge: Judson Press, 1976), pp. 43–44. Indeed, all these phrases are to be found in this excellent compendium of Black prayers.
7. An impressive number of articles on the topic of facing death has appeared recently in popular magazines. *Reader's Digest* 109, no. 652:81–84, published a *Family Circle* (September, 1975) article condensation under the title "When Face to Face with Death." This same article appeared also in the 24 November 1975, issue of *People*. "Coping with Death in the Family" was reprinted in an airline magazine from the 5 April 1975 issue of *Business Week*.
8. Richard N. Soulen, ed., "Epilogue," *Care for the Dying* (Atlanta: John Knox Press, 1976).
9. *The Hymnal of the Protestant Episcopal Church in the USA 1940* (New York: The Church Pension Fund, 1940), p. 564.

7. PREACHING AS DIALOGUE

1. Henry H. Mitchell, *Black Belief* (New York: Harper & Row, p. 46.
2. Thomas A. Johnson, "U.S. Blacks Tour Africa Slave Fort," New York Times, 23 July 1972, p. 6.
3. Henry H. Mitchell, *Black Preaching*, p. 106.
4. Sandy F. Ray, 24 June 1976, address at the Baptist Congress of Christian Education, San Francisco, California.
5. Henry H. Mitchell, "The Preaching Ministry to Blacks," *Military Chaplains' Review* 1, no. 1 (January 1972): 1–19.

8. TOWARD THE RECOVERY OF PREACHING

1. Anthropologists with special interest in the urban Black ghetto have confirmed this many times over. Works such as Carol B. Stack's *All Our Kin* (New York: Harper & Row, 1974) and Elliott Liebow's *Tally's Corner* (Boston: Little, Brown, 1967) are good examples of this finding of ad hoc family structures in the survival patterns of the Black and very poor.
2. Henry Sloan Coffin was President and Professor of Practical Theology at the Union Theological Seminary in New York City, having previously served as the Pastor of the Madison Avenue Presbyterian Church.
3. James W. English, *The Prophet of Wheat Street* (Elgin, Ill.: David C. Cook, 1967, 1973), p. 35.
4. Ibid., p. 76.

Index